FLORENCE ALLSHORN

FLORENCE ALLSHORN

and the
Story of St Julian's

J. H. OLDHAM

SCM PRESS LTD
BLOOMSBURY STREET
LONDON

First published October 1951
Reprinted February 1952

Printed in Great Britain by
The Camelot Press Ltd.,
London and Southampton

CONTENTS

PREFACE

FOR MORE than a quarter of a century I was in a position which brought me into close touch with most of the home administrators of the missionary societies in Great Britain, North America and the Continent of Europe, and with many of the leading missionaries in the various mission-fields of Asia and Africa. Among those whom I came to know in this way Florence Allshorn was one of the most remarkable. She saw further than most into the meaning of the missionary task and the nature of its demands. I welcomed every opportunity of learning from her wisdom. My colleague and successor in the secretaryship of the International Missionary Council, William Paton, formed a similar estimate of her qualities. 'Miss Allshorn?' he once remarked when her name was mentioned, 'I think she has the greatest spiritual insight of anyone I have ever known.'

But it was not only in missionary circles that her qualities won recognition. The impression she made on one who met her only casually is described in a letter from Miss Athene Seyler, the well-known actress. 'I only met Florence Allshorn', she writes, 'a few times—over a supper table, at a bazaar, in church. Each time I had an unforgettable and almost incommunicable impression of something I had never encountered before, a feeling that she was living in two worlds simultaneously, mine and one she brought with her. This seemed to show itself in a strange and delightful contradiction in her personality. She was at once gay and yet profoundly serious around her gaiety. She appreciated and offered the best of material pleasures and comforts and beauties and yet one suspected that they really meant nothing to her. She looked ready to share one's most trivial or sordid experience and one knew she would be untouched by it at the same time as bearing it. She gave me the impression of toughness

7

and delicacy, like silver wire. I believe, of course, that I am trying
to describe saintliness.'

The life of Florence Allshorn was spent in the main in the
service of Christian missions, but the story of it may upset a
good many preconceived notions of what a missionary is like.
The love of Christ was the ruling passion of her life, but the
expression of it was in no way conventional. She had in her life-
time the art of making friends with all sorts of people professing
a diversity of beliefs. If this book finds readers among those who
do not call themselves Christians, some of them, perhaps, in
spite of differences of outlook and language, will recognize in
her life an adventure of the human spirit that is directly related to
major decisions which to-day confront mankind as a whole, and
which are the common concern of all who care about its future.

That the writing of her life should have fallen to me came about
in this way. When I was staying at St Julian's at the beginning of
the present year, Florence Allshorn showed me a first draft of
some chapters of a small book about the St Julian's adventure,
and asked for my help in putting it into shape. We fixed a date
when I would spend a week at St Julian's and we would work on
the book together. Before the time came her last illness had begun.
After her death her colleagues asked me to complete the task.
When we looked into the matter we agreed that there must be a
biography of her and that the best course would be to combine it
with the story which she had nearly completed before her
death. The chapters written by Florence Allshorn herself form
Part II of this book. They are only a first rough draft and she
would doubtless have revised them considerably if she had
lived, but apart from a few necessary minor changes it seemed
best to print them as they came from her hand.

The members of the St Julian's Community and other friends
of Florence Allshorn have put on paper their recollections of her
for my use, and, in order to give unity to the narrative and to
avoid excessive quotation, have allowed me freely to incorporate,
with relatively little change, what they have contributed, without
specific acknowledgement. They have also allowed me to read
hundreds of her letters covering a period of more than thirty years.
Her letters were of the kind that people keep. I have also had the

opportunity of going carefully through a first draft of the present book with a small circle of those who were closest to her.

When references to other persons occur in quotations from her letters, an initial letter is used in place of the full name and, to avoid the risk of mistaken identification, the letter chosen is different from that of the actual name.

In addition to the unstinted help given me by members of the Community and other friends of Florence Allshorn, I have to thank my friends Dr Kathleen Bliss and Brother George Every for their kindness in reading in typescript a first draft of the book, and giving me advice and suggestions from which I have greatly benefited. The responsibility for what appears in this volume is, however, mine alone.

I have also to thank Messrs Martin Secker and Warburg for permission to quote from a poem by Edna St Vincent Millay and the editors of the *International Review of Missions* for allowing me to reproduce part of an article which appeared in that journal.

The publication of the book would have been delayed for many months if my wife had not assisted me in sorting out the material, typed the whole manuscript once and considerable portions of it twice, and given me help in many other ways.

J. H. O.

December, 1950.

PART I

FLORENCE ALLSHORN

I

EARLY YEARS

THE LIFE which flowered with singular splendour and frag-
rance in Florence Allshorn had an inauspicious beginning. She
was left an orphan at the age of three. Her father was a homeo-
pathic doctor who settled in the East End of London. He had
married a Miss Whitehead, a member of a well-to-do business
family in Sheffield. Four years after his marriage Dr Allshorn
died, leaving three children, Malcolm, Florence and Leo. The
strain of being the wife of a struggling doctor and of caring for a
young family was too much for Mrs Allshorn, and after returning to Sheffield she developed tuberculosis and died at the
age of twenty-six, when the three children were four, three
and two years old. Florence had been born on December 19th,
1887.

A Miss Jackson, who had been governess to the Whitehead
family and devoted to Mrs Allshorn, assumed the guardianship
of the children and brought them up in her own home. It seems
to have been a home without brightness. Miss Jackson had a kind
heart and plenty of common sense, was active in good works and
was superintendent of the Sunday School for many years. But
she was undemonstrative—Florence never remembered being
kissed by her. The religion in the home appears to have had a
somewhat narrow outlook. The surroundings of Florence's
childhood, as a cousin recalls them, were colourless and drab.
'I didn't enjoy youth', Florence herself wrote in later years. 'I
hated my home, it held me so tightly, and I was only happy in
escaping from it, which is a very dangerous thing to be brought
up on.'

The boys when they were of a suitable age were sent to a boarding-school and Florence was left at home alone. She went for a time to a day-school in Sheffield. The most direct way to it lay through a cemetery, and in the winter evenings the walk through the cemetery was something that tried her courage. All through her life she felt a sympathy for people who were afraid of the dark and of going out alone at night. The children saw little of their relations. The cousins were all so well dressed that Florence went through the agony of feeling shabby when she met them and of lacking most of the advantages which the rest of her mother's family seemed to enjoy. For the last two years of her school education she was sent to a small boarding-school at Pocklington.

There was something in Florence which kept her from succumbing to her environment. She had an independent spirit, and lived her own life of colour and excitement, of adventure and thought, in the midst of gloomy surroundings. She always loved creating things and at school did well in art and music.

After leaving school she went to the school of art in Sheffield. This she greatly enjoyed. She did well and her work was warmly commended. Unfortunately her eyes began to trouble her and she had to give up all work and live for six months in almost complete darkness with her eyes heavily shaded. There was a fear that she might lose her eye-sight altogether. But the six months rest brought a great improvement, though throughout her life her eyes continued to give her trouble. When she recovered, she took a four years course at the Sheffield School of Domestic Science, including cooking, laundry, house-wifery, needlework, dressmaking and psychology, and obtained a first-class diploma in all subjects. She inclined to think in later life that a training in art and domestic science was as good a training for life as any one could have. It taught one to *look* at things, trained the capacity of appreciation, encouraged a sense of proportion, and developed one's creative powers.

Throughout this period she continued to live with Miss Jackson. An exciting holiday, spent partly in Denmark, was made possible by a small legacy from her mother, which came to her on attaining the age of twenty-one.

In 1913 an event occurred which was a turning point in her life. Dr Gresford Jones was appointed Vicar and Archdeacon of Sheffield. Florence got to know him and Mrs Gresford Jones, and they became from that time onwards one of the greatest influences in her life. The following year Miss Dorothy Arnold, now Mrs Sargisson, became a member of the Cathedral staff, and she and Florence quickly became close friends. Another life-long friendship begun at this time was with the Rev Henry Cecil, then a member of the Cathedral staff and until recently Vicar and Rural Dean of Shoreditch, and Mrs Cecil. These friendships opened up something in her that went on growing till the day of her death. To her new friends she gave all the love and devotion that had been stored up through the years. Apart from her brother Leo there had been no one till then for whom she deeply cared. It now seemed as though springs of affection had been released in her and her friendships increased in many directions.

She was brought into the heart of church work. She was particularly successful in dealing with girls. She started a club for factory girls which reached a membership of more than eighty. 'My first memory of her', writes Bishop Gresford Jones, 'is at the centre of a group of rough factory girls. No one had been really able to reach them before, when lo! the miracle had happened, and there was this gay company in the parish hall, as happy as could be, and Florence the soul of it all'.

She gave her utmost for these girls. She had the power to get the best out of them, to tame their wildnesses and to make them love her, often with a great and lasting love. 'She did in fact', writes an old club girl, 'inspire every girl with her intense love of beauty, not only to look at, but beauty of mind and thought; and everything we did had to be of the very best'.

She also became superintendent of the girls' Sunday School. 'I remember', writes her friend Mrs Sargisson, 'how the children loved her at once, from the girls of fourteen and fifteen—a difficult age—down to the tiny mites. One ragged little scrap of about five used to follow her wherever she went. He seldom spoke. He just trotted along behind her from class to class, perfectly happy as long as she was within sight.'

For a year or two during this period she worked in a coal

office belonging to a cousin, and followed on paper the movements of trucks of coal all over England. She discovered that she
possessed an unusual memory. She rarely needed to look up files
when details were wanted; she seemed to remember them all.

In 1918 Florence was appointed a full time member of the
Cathedral staff, and the range of her activities increased. She
conducted a girls' Bible Class with more than sixty members.
She visited in the parish and hospitals. She took an active part in
promoting interest in foreign missions. Most of her spare time
she spent in reading. She had a taste for novels, which remained
with her throughout her life, but her chief interest lay in biography, books dealing with current social problems and works of
religion and theology. She mentions in a letter that she is deep in
Evelyn Underhill's *The Mystic Way*, and says that she 'read till
my head hummed—goodness, it is a book!' She was especially
attracted by the writings of Olive Schreiner and was greatly
influenced, in particular, by her book *Dreams*, which she read and
re-read until she knew it almost by heart.

Mrs Sargisson has drawn a picture of her as she was in those
Sheffield days:

> She touched life at many points. She was one of the out-
> standing students at the School of Art and the School of
> Domestic Science. She loved music and accompanied from
> sight with ease. She had a natural facility for any pursuit that
> came her way. I remember when she first handled a golf
> club her companion refused to believe she had never played
> before. When mountaineering, the guide quickly saw she did
> not need his help. 'She is like a goat, that one,' he remarked.
> When she had her first riding lesson she was obviously entirely
> at home in the saddle. She seemed to know instinctively the
> right way to handle both things and people.
>
> I don't think I have ever known anyone with quicker
> perceptions. She had an unerring eye for beauty in any form.
> We covered half Derbyshire in our long walks over the heather,
> Florence always the first to note a specially lovely bit of moor-
> land or sky.
>
> They were joyous days in spite of much that was difficult,
> with laughter always near the surface. With her quick free
> eager spirit she was an ideal companion. Her sense of fun and

readiness to laugh at herself were delightful, especially when allied to self-discipline. One day I noticed her wearing an unusually shabby pair of shoes. 'Aren't they dreadful?' she said cheerfully. 'It's because I've just done a bad thing and whenever I behave like that again I'm going to wear my very oldest shoes as a punishment.'

Florence's brother Malcolm went to Australia to farm. He died at a comparatively early age. Her younger brother Leo, of whom she was very fond, reacted against the atmosphere of the home and broke away from religion, at least for a time. He went to Cambridge, where he took a good degree and became a historian of promise. But he developed tuberculosis and died at an early age.

At the beginning of 1920 Florence decided to offer herself for missionary service abroad, and got into touch with the Church Missionary Society. She gave as her reason that she wanted to serve Jesus Christ in the best way that she could and believed that her life would count for more abroad than at home. The Archdeacon of Sheffield in commending her to the Church Missionary Society, expressed the hope that it 'would lay hold of her with both hands.' A month or two later Bishop Willis of Uganda visited Sheffield and a talk with him convinced Florence that that was the field in which she was called to serve. Archdeacon Gresford Jones and his wife decided at the same time to offer themselves for service in Uganda.

Fortunately a good many letters written by Florence while she was at Sheffield still survive. The following extracts give us a glimpse of the way she saw life at this time. It is striking how many of the thoughts characteristic of her later years appear here in germ.

She quotes a poem of Walt Whitman and comments:

I do think you get that great exultation of living more on the sea than anywhere. Riding's nearly as great. I want both and can't have either. Oh d———! ...

When I look back, my heart is so full of joy to feel how Christ has gripped me all through. And these last few weeks have been so happy because I've felt Him so surely turning me

B

towards Him. He knows there's never been anything I've wanted half so much as that.

To a friend who was on holiday:

Don't worry your head about theological problems. Read books with only half-a-dozen lines on a page, mostly sloppy. It will do you a world of good. Also, don't think about yourself at all, I mean your moral self. Just be a pagan, loving the sky and the sun and the smell of things and let yourself expand that way a bit. It's no end healthy. 'Come clear of the nets of right and wrong'—do! I'm sure I'm talking sense. You'll be twice as effective and clear-sighted when you come home. Do you know I think one of the best things you can do on holiday is to ask nothing, want nothing, but just praise God for everything. Always be praising Him—for the little sticky leaves, the rich sombre greenness of the trees, all the kindness you get, on a holiday. Just one long praise of little beautiful things and forget that great, big, striving, blundering self of yours. Then come back to us clean and fresh and contagious and let us too get a sight of the glory of God.

How full life is and we're touching just a tiny, tiny wave of it, and it's as big as a sea to us. And the sovereignty of the mind—isn't it a treasure trove, bottomless simply?

There isn't such a thing as defeat. There are only the great simple victories of life—to love strongly, to seek strongly and to be strongly happy, and perhaps that's the most difficult of them all.

Reason is such a stolid thing to guide by. It never told any one to pitch himself into a failing battle. It never told a Christ to make the sins of others His burden, nor a man to make the purity of other men his agonizing endeavour. Reason tells you to do such dreadfully sensible things, and intuition is the glamour of God's life in you that makes you do the high, foolish things and puts the lilt of God's singing into your heart —or else why are you so suddenly mad with joy over nothing at all?

I saw dimly just now, I think truly for the first time, how the world needs the gentleness and sweetness and clearness of Christ. It makes the whole hard fixity of things break up and lie tender and trembling. How *is* it possible that there can ever be times when I slip along heedless of God. There are always such times—with me, they are my great sin, and they glide coldly over that great 'want' that is always within me. These are the things that daunt you—the shallows of yourself. Still I'm not going to be daunted. I'm out for the hazard again. Is it so impossible to live up to your utmost? I'll dare to try.

You see there's this human side of you that loves and sees the need of loving and caring and wants to help so badly— so badly that you want to leave all the other far-away heavenly side of you. And then there's this other side that simply cannot leave go of you, and it comes over you that you are, no matter what, a thing apart with a spirit aching to grow. I don't think I can make you understand what I understand so little myself. Only I must hold on to the love of God and listen to His voice till my soul becomes filled with the one supreme thing. Then I can come to you and bring to you such a much more perfect friendship, something that will be infinitely more worth having, because it has stood in the wide places of the wilderness and troubled a little.

I think my sin is aimlessness, but it's difficult to know what to aim at. I do want to justify my existence. There's such a zest in life just now. I feel life's just starting again. I believe I shall all my life be chucking up the old things and going in for new, because it's so invigorating pelting into the unknown, and I believe I shall always be falling out of the frying pan into the fire. And God save me from ever settling down.

I want a lot of things for you, but they aren't things that come easy. I don't want results for you, or nice things even. It's so difficult to say what I want. I think it's a bigger reverence for yourself—knowledge that you can't stoop to a littleness of thought or deed.

Wouldn't you go through anything to be able to creep a little nearer to His feet? I still ache so for life. The things that stir you to the soul, all the clean, pure, beautiful things of God's earth—they are heaven to me. All these years I have climbed absolutely alone. Is it any wonder I haven't got far. Now I have you to climb with and it's good.

I do honestly feel there is nothing to be compared with the Christian life. It's so extraordinary the way religion grips you. I've been thinking of the martyrs and how they died, because they wouldn't give it up—*they couldn't*, it was in their very blood. It's *yourself*, you couldn't pluck it out, so they really died because they wouldn't tell or live a lie or dishonour God.

I hate being weak when what's needed is strength. I hate being ineffective when it's leaders that the world is wanting. I *hate, hate, hate* being ordinary and just nice but dull. This world can't be all, or you couldn't want so much that you'll never get. You couldn't live these dead lives if you weren't going to be alive sometime.

Let's pray hard for each other. I want courage more than anything, I think. Oh, I don't know. I want to *see* God, that's everything. Do get it for me—I believe in your prayers so much.

I'm certain that work done perfectly for the pure love of it, like an art work, like our work, any work, can't perish—perfect things can't. But when you get self into it, it's not perfect and it's not strong enough to live. I believe that trampling self under foot is the only test for entering the ranks of the 'eternal priests'.

I *don't* like the idea of God as a fairy godmother. He's a million times more sublime than my sublimest thought of Him. He's the Lord of a beautiful, pure and high sanctuary in my soul and sometimes, because I'm so wistful about it, I get a glimpse of the loftiness of it, and sometimes I imagine Him with no form at all, but love and tenderness and a great calling going in front of me, and I don't see how I can ever do anything but follow. And I'm not content with goodness and niceness and duty which I have struggled for. Now I want Him, touching and speaking to me, hurting me, and I loving Him. Words are beautiful things, and thoughts and knowledge, but I'm starving and they're no use to me. I know what I want as I've never known anything in my life, and how I'm to stumble through the mistakes and the limitations to it is too hard for me. Surely God knows how thirsty I am. I want to have power and be of use, and have you not to be on the heights yourself before you can drag anyone there? I don't feel I'll be the least use until I have got Christ *in* me, and perhaps I'll seek and seek for that all my life. Things aren't easy, are they?

I am so troubled about not loving people enough. Perhaps God will teach me to love, if I ask hard enough. I feel somehow as if I'm not awake yet. I feel as though there is such lots more in me that somehow hasn't got a releasing touch yet. I do want to come awake, only I don't know how. You remember when I had my teeth out and altogether did have a good deal of pain —well I found myself thanking God for that because it was *real*, and it taught me depths. I quite exulted over it afterwards. It was as though I had found one part at least of me that was *real*. And I want to feel like that about every single thing. Perhaps it's pain or some big disaster that will do it. I hope I shall have enough courage if it is, and I want to have enough courage to *want* it even. I daren't yet.

I used to think there was something in me that was too precious to run the risk of mixing with ugly, ordinary things— a kind of mystical dream of something that might grow into something very beautiful, if I kept my mind up in the clouds enough and did not allow it to be soiled. I can't explain it, but it was purely selfish. And now I know that life is clean, dirty, ugly, beautiful, wonderful, sordid—and above all love. Just fancy, I even used to think I was rather good at that. I used to think that being nice to people and feeling nice was loving people. But it isn't, it isn't. Love is the most immense unselfishness and it's so big I've never touched it.

II

MISSIONARY TO UGANDA

MISS ALLSHORN was accepted by the Church Missionary Society, who decided to send her out without further training, and at the age of thirty-two she sailed for Uganda in 1920 with a large party of missionaries, including Bishop and Mrs Gresford Jones, the Archdeacon having been consecrated assistant-bishop of Kampala.

The story of the planting of the Church in Uganda is one of the most romantic in the history of modern missions. The lives of the martyred Bishop Hannington and of Alexander Mackay, the young Scottish engineer, described by Lord Rosebery as 'that Christian Bayard', were at the turn of the century among the classics of missionary literature. In 1875 H. M. Stanley had arrived in Uganda and written his historic letter to the *Daily Telegraph*, in which he said that 'Nowhere is there in all the pagan world a more promising field for a mission than Uganda.' The Church Missionary Society responded immediately to the appeal. Money poured in, and in 1877 a party of eight missionaries was sent out. The climate and the hardships of travel took a heavy toll of the party, and of those who set out only two arrived in Mengo. Within forty years nearly a third of the population had become professing Christians. This had come about largely through the conversion of leading chiefs, who brought their followers with them into the Church. Florence was to discover how superficial much of the christianization was. But outwardly there was a large and vigorous Christian community, including many of the leading men in the country and proud of its roll of martyrs, European and African.

Florence Allshorn was sent on her arrival to the station of
Iganga in Busoga. The climate of the Busoga country is excep-
tionally unhealthy. In the early days Bishop Tucker had written
that in Busoga all nature seemed to be suffering from limpness
and lack of energy; and that under these enervating conditions
not only the body, but the mind also, was apt to suffer. Bishop
Gresford Jones writes that

perhaps nowhere else in Uganda is this psychic pressure of evil
to be felt in anything like the same degree. You have only to
sit alone on the verandah in the short African twilight, when the
mind is receptive to impressions, to feel this ominous, un-
accountable shadow that preys upon life. It is not difficult then
to imagine how in the beautiful, evergreen forests, below the
rank mass of undergrowth, something real and sinister is
urging those cruel, tightly-clinging creepers to choke slowly and
surely the life out of the trees to which they cling; that in this
chill, penetrating miasma rising from the swamps is something
heavy and malevolent, ready to weave into the minds and
souls of the people its web of abominable emotions.[1]

Seven young missionaries had been sent to the Iganga station
in as many years, and none had been willing to stay. The difficulty
was not only the debilitating and nerve-racking effect of the
climate, but also the temperament of the senior woman missionary. She was of the pioneer type and very wiry. She had quelled
single-handed attacks of plague by burning down whole villages,
and she ruled her kingdom with an arm of steel. She gave herself
to the people and expected others to do the same. She was
impervious to the newer ideas about missionary work that were
stirring in the minds of younger missionaries. She had come out
to save the souls of the heathen, and save them she would, even
if it meant pursuing a malefactor round and round the table with
a stick, or that no one had been able in past years to live with
her. When Florence arrived she found the one and only sitting-
room divided into two halves. In the one was cramped together
all the senior's furniture; the other half was entirely bare. 'That's
your half,' she was informed.

[1] *Uganda in Transformation*, pp. 87-8.

Though Florence did not know a word of the language, she was put in charge of the girls' school, a 'High School for Chiefs' Daughters', the pupils of which knew no English. The other missionary went on her own way, dispensing and visiting and left Florence to sink or swim in the school. Florence's impressions on reaching Iganga are given in her first letter from that station:

Busoga at last, and it *is* a job! It's *the* girls' boarding school for the whole of Busoga. No one can speak English, and the only other European lady is the worker among the women and in the dispensary. She's nervy, and the lady whose place I am taking has gone dicky with her nerves. So I am in the soup. But it's a *great* job, because it's the place on which the raising of the status of the women of Busoga depends. Isn't that a gorgeous bit of work to tackle? I'm jolly glad of it. Thank God for something absolutely impossible.

From the beginning to the end of her stay in Uganda Florence's keen eyes were directed with equal steadiness and perspicacity to the good and the evil in her surroundings; she responded with her whole being to all that was lovely and enjoyable and, when sorrow and suffering came to her, she looked them in the face and did not shrink from the encounter. She knew the truth of William Blake's lines

> *Man was made for Joy and Woe;*
> *And when this we rightly know,*
> *Thro' the World we safely go,*
> *Joy and woe are woven fine,*
> *A clothing for the soul divine.*

Three or four weeks after her arrival she writes of Iganga as 'a lovely spot' and tells of a party the girls in the school gave her on her birthday. They all sat round two lanterns on the floor in the long, dark schoolroom, and the girls danced and sang. Florence thinks that she could make her fortune if she were able to bring the whole show to London. In another letter written about the same time she writes:

I need God so much here. *Everything* is so difficult. There is so much 'ungoodness' in everything. I keep reminding myself that I am here for Christ and that all the wild and miserable things as well as the holy and calm ones must beat through me if I am to be used at all. And I thank God I am here and that it isn't easy. I always wanted that.

In spite of all discouragements and difficulties, she writes at the end of eight months, 'I am beginning to love my work; if I had a pal to talk it over with I'd be as happy as the day is long.' And towards the close of her first year she says, 'One year nearly gone—I've enjoyed everything, really it's been really living.'

Florence always believed that 'experience', good or bad, was the thing to covet, because through it one grew. Her first year in Uganda had been full of experiences of all sorts. In the school she found her girls 'quite as difficult as English club girls, but just as lovable.' They were

suspicious, half-devil, half-child, slothful, irresponsive, slow. The Musoga isn't like the Muganda even; the latter does want to learn, the former *doesn't* as a rule. Can you imagine forty-two girls none of them *wanting* to learn anything (yes, two do)? Can you imagine me with my quick way of doing things having to wait every time I call a girl, while I speak at least three times before she attempts to heed, then looks at me for some time, then slowly rises and comes to me? I want to get behind and kick and kick! You've no idea how hard it is. Then can you imagine telling them time after time to keep things clean and no one attempts to do it unless I'm on the spot *all the time*? Can you imagine making a rule that the big girls are to watch the little ones' toes—and after leaving the prefects to watch that rule to call an inspection one day and find some mites with as many as fifteen jiggers in? And you thunder at the big ones and they all turn sulky and you can't do a thing with them. To find how to manage them is so big a problem that most people despair and don't try. But I *do* want to. And I do love 'em all so I want to get at the bottom of things frightfully.

As regards life in general, she writes a few weeks after her arrival:

Well what with all this loneliness, disheartening work, language, rats in your bedroom, lots of them, hyaenas, leopards and jackals in the garden, keeping you awake half the night more often than not, another seven foot black snake outside my bedroom door, ants, bites by the hundred, you've simply got to grip on to all the courage you possess and fight and fight not to get under it all. The queer thing is that I have really been happier this month than I have ever been before; you get driven back and back on God every time.

A month or two later she was coping with an outbreak of plague and says, after the worst was over:

It isn't so much the work itself that gets on top of one, but the bother, jealousy among the matrons, quarrels, keeping houses in repair and wages up and so little money, making ends meet all round, the struggle of keeping your own mind up, surrounded as you are with such low level thinking—you can hardly realize what that is, and the drag of it,—without any of the help you get from people like you at home.

Far the most acute struggle for Florence, however, was in the sphere of relations with her fellow-missionaries. She had written shortly before leaving Sheffield that love was something so big that she had never touched it. By far the most important event in her four years in Uganda was that she was brought face to face with the meaning of love. The question engaged her attention almost as soon as she reached the country. Writing about a fellow-missionary, (not her senior colleague at Iganga), who had proved unequal to the test, she says:

Things were too hard for her. But I'm harder, not having had too easy a time ever. Besides when you burrow down, you generally find people don't *want* to be beastly. It's generally because *they* have been hit so hard and are so disappointed with life. I always want to butt in and get them to see straight, don't you? Your silly self gets hurt at first. Then, when you come round, it's great fun trying to do it. Human nature is so enthralling, and, if people are catty, *there's a reason*.

But it was on her own station at Iganga that the battle had to be fought and won. We have seen that her senior colleague was not an easy person to live with. Florence describes the situation in a letter written a few months after her arrival:

My colleague is a dear in some ways, but the matter of fact is that Iganga is a hopeless sort of place. Of the people who have had my job before no one has stayed more than a few months, because it's so unhealthy and has made them all ill. My colleague has stuck it; it just happens not to have affected her health, but it has absolutely rotted her nerves, and she has the most dreadful fits of temper. Sometimes she doesn't speak at all for two days. Just now we've finished up three weeks of never a decent word or smile.

Florence describes her predicament in another letter:

You see the horrid thing is that I can't speak the language, so I am dependent on her. I have to ask her things and bring things to her every hour of the day. If it wasn't for that I could just keep to myself till it's over more or less. There are two things I want you to pray for hard. One is the language. The other is that I may keep pitiful. It's bearable then and I can help to haul her through these times, but when I get resentful and horrid it's just unbearable. Don't think it's always bad. She is just as nice as I said she was, and while I was bad she was never cross once. But it does seem queer, it could be such a happy home. I seem fated not to have a decent home, don't I? You can see what a tough thing it is for the girls too. I am sure it isn't the right thing just to leave her to it. I've got to try to haul her through. But oh, if it wasn't only that, if there wasn't the language and the loneliness and feeling slack and other things. *Don't* think I am unhappy. I am not, honestly. I think I am a good one for the job, because I am not used to a 'calm' home. Only do pray God to keep near me and to keep me gentle and loving in my thoughts. It's no use being loving only when people are nice.

Florence was brought almost to the point of despair. She felt that she had reached the limit of her endurance. It seemed clear to her that she might as well go back to England for all the good that she was doing. She was not bringing the spirit of Jesus Christ into the school; the children were fully aware that the atmosphere was wrong. She had come to the crisis of her life. The story of it may be given in her own words.

I was young and I was the eighth youngster who had been sent, none of whom had lasted more than two years. I went down to seven stone and my spirit and soul wilted to the same degree. Then one day the old African matron came to me when I was sitting on the verandah crying my eyes out. She sat at my feet and after a time she said, 'I have been on this station for fifteen years and I have seen you come out, all of you saying you have brought to us a Saviour, but I have never seen this situation saved yet.' It brought me to my senses with a bang. I was the problem for myself. I knew enough of Jesus Christ to know that the enemy was the one to be loved before you could call yourself a follower of Jesus Christ, and I prayed, in great ignorance as to what it was, that this same love might be in me, and I prayed as I have never prayed in my life for that one thing. Slowly things rightened. Whereas before she had been going about upsetting everybody with long deep dreadful moods, and I had been going into my school depressed and lifeless, both of us found our way to lighten each other. She had a great generosity and I must have been a cruel burden to her, worn out as she was. But I did see that as we two drew together in a new relation the whole character of the work on the station altered. We had some little real love to show to the people on it; they were freer with us, and less uneasy of what sort of attitude they would meet in us when they came. It is a long story and I could not put in half here, and it reads as though I had been the great reconciler. But that is certainly not true. She had been beaten in that place, and I was only in the process of being beaten, and the old matron saved me.

Something had happened to Florence so profound that she never found it easy to speak of it. She decided to stay—and to love, and to let Christ save the situation through her.

I suddenly realized [she once told a friend] that it didn't matter two hoots what happened to me; the only thing that mattered was what happened to God and the other person. From that moment everything changed. I stopped bothering about myself. And, though it often wasn't easy, we came to fashion a good working sort of friendship. We both enjoyed books and could share many together. Gradually the whole atmosphere of the place altered. The children felt it and began to share in it, and to do little brave unselfish things that they had never done before.

For a whole year Florence read the thirteenth chapter of the first Epistle to the Corinthians every day. Life became an adventure in learning to love instead of the agony it had been before. The older missionary became very fond of Florence, and Florence was able to write in later letters of 'my colleague whom I have come to love very much indeed'. When her furlough came in sight and she was discussing the likelihood of her returning to Uganda she said, 'It has been the best "home" I've ever known. My colleague has made it that for me this last year.'

It was the spiritual regeneration that Florence experienced in Uganda that was the fount of all that she taught in later years to successive generations of missionaries. When she talked to them about 'love' she knew what it meant and what it costs. Her dearly bought experience gave meaning to every sentence in such a passage as the following from a talk which she gave on the eve of her last illness:

To love a human being means to accept him, to love him as he is. If you wait to love him till he has got rid of his faults, till he is different, you are only loving an idea. He is as he is now, and he is to be loved now, as he is; I can only love a person by allowing myself to be disturbed by him as he is. I must accept the pain of seeing him with hopefulness and expectancy that he can be different. To love him with the love of Christ means first of all to accept him as he is, and then try to lead him towards a goal he doesn't see yet—and because I love, to attack all that is contrary to God with all the energy of love. Christ's love is exactly like that; it is entirely disinterested and selfless; it accepts you as you are, with all that is displeasing, disappointing and even painful for Him in you; it gives love whatever the response may be; it forgives and forgives endlessly.

When her old students wrote to her, telling her of very difficult conditions, she used often to write back: 'Good, this is your chance, don't miss it.' But while the conception of life as challenge and response was central to all her thinking, her faith in the power of love to triumph over every obstacle was combined with a shrewd insight into people and situations. She knew that the challenge was not always met; that not all were capable of meeting it. 'It is not fair', she would sometimes say in regard to some one whom she knew to be immature, 'to expose her to that situation'.

In spite of the climate, ill-health and the problem of personal relations, Florence did a first-class job in the school. She brought her keen intelligence to bear on her task and was sufficiently free from restrictions to be able to run the school as she thought best. Gardening had a much larger place in the curriculum than was usual in most schools, since it helped to meet what was at the time the most urgent need of the community. The Phelps-Stokes Education Commission which visited Uganda in 1924 referred in its Report to the 'first-rate girls' boarding school' at Iganga, and described it as 'a particularly good piece of work'. This was high praise from a Commission of experienced educators, the Chairman of which was Dr Thomas Jesse Jones, a leading authority on Negro education in the United States, who had previously visited West Africa as chairman of a similar educational commission.

Florence gave an account of the school in an article published after her return from Africa:

There is a girls' boarding school here of about 100 girls, of ages from 5 to 20. There is no work so fascinating as managing a boarding school. Think what it means to have the children on the spot, to be able to learn the characteristics of each child, to teach it regularly, to give it definite training in cleanliness, to discipline it, and to see the wonder of the beginnings of its own self-discipline. You have only to work for a short time in a day school to see the far greater chance there is in a boarding school. Not the least important is the out-of-school life of the girl, where in her cooking, in the bedroom, and in her leisure she is made to feel the responsibility of life, to rub off her selfish edges against the needs of others, and above all to learn the great law of love and the helping of those who need her help.

In my own school I put each small child into the care of a
senior girl; she is made to be responsible for the health and
good behaviour of the child who is in her charge. At first
this led to tumultuous happenings. An outraged senior would
be seen dragging a small rebellious junior to my verandah.
'This child fails me', she would say with a world of exasperation
in her voice. 'She will not obey, she refuses to do anything I
tell her!' It was difficult to believe, seeing the small meek figure
on her knees there; but I was very solemn and pointed out to
her the wickedness of disobedience in what I hoped was an
impressive manner. The tumult having subsided for the
moment, I watched them go back down the curving path, the
senior with her head high and offended dignity still written all
over her, and the junior trotting behind trying to look properly
chastened, but also, one secretly felt, trying hard not to put out
her tongue at that majestic figure in front.

There is also a teachers' training class of from twenty to
thirty girls. These latter, beside their theoretical training, get
practical training by taking classes in the school itself and
having a criticism class once a week. Then they go out to
village centres and manage a day school for girls. Naturally,
at first they are very feeble and their ingrained mental lethargy
is always a desperate thing to fight, so that they need regular
supervision and visiting. But it is difficult for the one woman to
do it all—school, training class, and long-distance visits on a
push-bike—though there never was such need as there is now
in Busoga for thorough treaching and individual treatment.

Busoga is a country that pulls at the heart-strings. Only the
power of God is sufficient for it, but that is sufficient, combined
with all the compassion and understanding love we can give.
Against a very dark background there are brilliant sparks, a
girl and a woman there, fighting with her back to the wall—
fighting with a tenacious faith in her Lord that is an amazement
to us who watch, and surely an earnest of what we may hope
shall be.[1]

In one of Florence's annual letters to the Church Missionary
Society there occurs a passage which reveals the insight, patience
and faith of the true educator—qualities which were to find
outstanding expression in her later work of training missionaries.

[1] *Church Missionary Outlook,* August, 1925.

It is very difficult work [she writes], as it must be for all of us, to keep our impatient minds quiet enough to be fair to them and not to expect the impossible from them. The thought that keeps you going freshly, after all, is this that even in *their* infinitesimal thinking powers there are seeds growing—you see them rarely but you do see them; and that somewhere in each one, surely and certainly helping it on, is the vital image of God even stronger than their long deadening past and pushing upwards and onwards from a sure centre. So that in spite of the slowness of the progress you seem to make, it is a work fascinating in the extreme, and, too, full of hope always.

When her senior colleague went on furlough, Florence had to be responsible for the hospital as well as the school. The prospect seemed to her 'rather daunting. To be left on a station with no nurse and no doctor get-at-able is simply nerve-racking and such dreadful things come to the hospital and happen everywhere.'

Full as her hands were at Iganga, Florence's mind never ceased to range over problems of the Uganda mission as a whole. She knew that the difficulties she had encountered in her own station were common elsewhere.

I *have* met some ugly things [she writes]. I've never seen it so clearly before, and yet I believe there *is* a movement, people are recognizing how everybody else is hurting everybody else, but are apt not to recognize that they themselves are hurting anyone else; isn't it queer how blind we are? I myself am frankly frightened at what is ahead for me if I stay here. It seems to me I am always going to come up against these outrageous things and these *hard* natures which rouse all the bad in me. You haven't the same hatefulness of resentment in you, you couldn't understand how they make me so utterly wretched and intolerant myself, and you don't know where the righteous resentment leaves off and the other begins. Only I feel I have got to work that out and get through somehow and not just leave it. I would hate to feel I was letting it go on if I could do anything, and surely there *is* a way—there *is*. But not unless I can kill this intolerance in myself, and how can I do it anywhere but *here*; it hardly ever came up in me at home.

She writes to a friend at home:

I wish you were here to join in a rebellion against the suppression of individuality and the idea that you are servants of an institution rather than of God and of your own conscience.

The remark that she could not 'just leave it' is characteristic of her whole attitude. Wherever she saw that things were wrong her impulse was to step in and do something. The readiness to accept conflict instead of acquiescing in evil breathes all through her letters. About dealing with Africans she writes:

The African *can* learn, quickly too, and at bottom wants to learn, but to teach him you've got to be very just, very firm, very down on his faults, and *loving enough to bother about it all*. It's much easier to say, 'Oh, it's his custom, leave him alone'.

The sense of human littleness would often come over her. 'Oh, *do* ask God to save me from the pettiness there is here—it's one great web.' She describes the feeling evoked in her as she watched a sunset.

There was a great piled up mass of clouds with the sun setting behind them; a fighting sunset, but so grand, and I sat and wondered and wondered what *was* the meaning of things, and what is the meaning of us, tiny people with our huge faith—because it is a huge faith to believe what we believe. We're such scraps over against a sunset like that, that it doesn't *seem* as if it could matter what we are, or much what we did; and yet it matters so enormously. Why? It would be lovely *not* to matter and yet hateful, and everything is like that. The ache of God in you and the weariness of your denial of it—all bewildering and contradictory.

But in all her perplexities and discouragements Florence was sustained by the knowledge that she possessed the clue to all her problems. 'What everything needs here is to be deluged in love; *everything* wants loving.' And in another letter, 'Before we can hope to move things out here, I believe we have just got to be *living* I Corinthians 13. I am certain of it, I feel nothing else

C

matters in comparison at all, organizations, gifts of speech— *nothing*.'

She had attained to a serene confidence in the power of God to make love victorious.

I am always jolly glad about everything [she says] and I am an incurable optimist. I have seen such a lot of mistakes overruled and you feel always the guiding of things. I used to think other people had such a power to dish up your life, but in a way I don't think so now. I think if you love God with that queer patience and passion which comes with your love for Him, you get fundamentally out of the hands of men; they can alter your doings and beings but they can't prevent them. I mean the will of God will come through you in one way if not in another, and it's the most beautifully safe feeling.

Notwithstanding the happy change that had come about in her relations with her colleague, the strain of the work and of the climate of Iganga began to tell on her. 'If my letters aren't always what I would like them to be,' she writes, 'it is only the depressed Iganga mood that does it. You don't know what it is like.' And again, 'I'm tired of things being so *hard* for everybody, tired, *tired, tired*.' And a few weeks later:

I have not been keeping near to God. Your mind's so tired here, too tired to concentrate even on prayer. It's only when some really strong unhappiness comes, I think, that I really pray. I have had a jolly stiff time, and I expect I always shall, with my idiotic temperament. It's no good having one in Africa and among missionaries, I can tell you, and you just dash against maddening hard walls all the time.

She admits that the last year had been a nightmare. But her courage held out to the end. 'I always bump up smiling,' she writes towards the close of her stay, 'and everything is *experience*.' The month before she sailed she went one evening for a ride, and 'got caught in the biggest storm I have seen, even out here, I think. It was *glorious* dashing through it, I just revelled in it.' The thought of seeing England again helped to keep her going. 'However beautiful and grand Africa is, it isn't England. Sometimes when it's very quiet, a bird gives a little English chirp out of the thicket, and my heart goes scudding.' 'Oh for a long, lazy day on the moors again, when it won't just be dreaming of it, but I'll really be with it. Four years of longing for it burn and smart at the back of my eyes when I think of it, and a tiny bit of real ecstasy like deep music right inside me.' In the end she confesses, 'I shall be glad to get away. I am done.'

Two letters written towards the close of her stay in Uganda shed light on the kind of person Florence was—and was to be:

You seem to meet such heaps of nice people, while I seem to be having to try not to be wild with people here. I ought to be a beautiful character, but I am a beastly one. I expect when I get out I shall have forgotten to make friends. I could howl sometimes for a 'rag'. But never mind. I have done a lot since I came here—been an influence for good, learned to whack girls over the head with a plate or anything you have in your hand, lead in extempore prayer, cook beautifully, entertain, help at confinements, keep my head when I wanted to lose it, keep calm with an obnoxious insect the size of my hand down my back, to use my tongue, to think a theatre is the height of earthly bliss, to think men are poor worms and that the only hope is in women, to bear with a lofty patience the fact that people don't realize that I've given my young life up to them, to suffer fools gladly (perhaps), and oh a lot more. . . .

I have never much cared for the *way* I have had to live here. I just long sometimes to stop this 'doing' and 'be' for the people. I'm sure I personally have more influence that way. I'd like a place in a training home of some kind in England. How to find out what is in you that is usable and how to work it out in life seems to me to be the thing I have not yet found.

The second letter was written on the eve of her coming home:

I lay on my hot bed this afternoon and wallowed in the trough of hating littlenesses in myself. I have got to be bigger somehow—do something somehow *big*. Staying and coming back here could be big, because it's a rotten place—absolutely, but I can make it most awfully little too. Wanting and seeing bigness ought to *do* something. I can't bear to think I'm living in the little way. Such heaps of people do. I want something enormous, don't you? The only thing I can think of would be some big painful endurance like this has been, only I have not made it big.

I look towards going home as a most hopeful thing. I feel I'll find out things. I am years older, thank goodness. I *want* age. Youth is so excessive over things that really don't matter. It's glorious in a way, but I was always *mad* to learn things, and you only want things of experience, and you can't experience without age. Therefore I think you must always feel done out of it that you haven't had the experience of married love. But it's obviously not *the* necessary thing, and there are perhaps other experiences just as beautiful. Love, if it's *very* big, must have other experiences, whatever kind of love it is. Only I want to stay stretched up. It's crawling along the rut that hurts so. And I couldn't have borne many kinds of marriage. I'd always have had to be free—do you know what I mean?

I talk an awful lot of rot, don't I? But I am much more careful how I talk about religious things, because somehow I want a new view of it. And I don't want to start by being *told* things I ought to think or do. I want to get rid of all that, and get so straight and sincere that I shall see *truth*, and so find out Christ afresh. Because He haunts you, and you must always be finding Him afresh, one day you'll find Him so really that you'll be wild with joy always. (I'm fed up with unjoyful Christians.) I believe until I get that joy I won't really have found Him.

III

INTERLUDE

FLORENCE sailed from Uganda in November 1924 and dis-embarked at Genoa. With a friend she paid a brief visit to Florence. She describes a visit to the Uffizi Gallery:

We spent our time seeing Botticelli. The 'Madonna del Magnificat' enraptured me. I couldn't get a good print; they were good copies, but soulless absolutely. It was queer, when you looked first you thought what a badly shaped baby face and what beautiful faces the surrounding children have. Then when you looked at the Child's face a long, long time, and then back to the children's, the latter began to look quite flat and uninteresting. Then you went back again to the Child's face and you found that the real divine thing was in the eyes. *That* the prints can't give, so I didn't get one. I felt as if a real little bit of pure adoration was being born in me because I was *seeing* the thing that is generally so elusive. Isn't it bewildering when you think of what the uttermost beauty, religion, makes you do—spend your life in slums and dreadful mission halls with flaring gas jets, everything ugly, or out in Iganga with filthy habits and dreadful beds which sicken you to touch, and to have your eyes pinned down on those kind of things? And you get such tiny, tiny bits of real exaltation of soul, and it's so utterly heavenly when you do.

Florence reached England shortly before Christmas. She looked thin and wasted and her appearance was a shock to her friends. She had stayed too long in Africa. For the next few months she visited friends and attended meetings and conferences. But she never felt well.

37

Her impressions of England after four years of absence are
given in a letter written after a visit to Sheffield.

It's great to feel at anyrate that you make people look away
from Sheffield ruts and out over something wide and bigger.
I feel it quite tremendously important that I should be out there
again, but how I'll ever leave people again I can't think. I
come all over dithery when I think of it.

There is something quite different at home these days.
Things do seem to have slipped a little loose. No one seems to
do *much* that they don't want to do—there's no fanaticism that
does things. It rather bewilders one. There's an awful lot of
rather dreary not-happiness, perhaps not definitely unhappy but
un-joyfulness. What does 'Come out and be ye separate' mean?
It surely needn't be dull and pi and unloving. There should be
a separation that *is* severe, but is quick and passionate and
attractive too. I wonder if that's what the world wants. It is
frightfully weary over wanting something. It makes you ache
dreadfully. And one person's little giving is so pitifully absurd
in such a tremendous need. But we needn't get bowled over by
our aching or our bewilderment. Come back and back to 'Be
still and know that I am God,' and keep your courage steady;
that's it, isn't it?

Her thoughts turned frequently to Uganda, to which at that
time she expected to return.

Last night I sat up on the bottom of my bed for a long time, and
I thought of what I am *beginning* to learn, I think—learn so
slowly, through you: that there is this royal inward happiness,
which can shine in the midst of a thousand things that make for
unhappiness; that a few tired, depressed moods *can't* defeat it,
so that we needn't *fear* Iganga ever any more; that pity can heal
any bitterness, and that we can ask for and get abundantly this
divine and human gospel of *patience* in dealing with people and
things. And these things you do bring me, because you bring
me back to where I can find them in Christ.

After she had been the best part of a year in England, Florence
was persuaded to see a specialist. He discovered that she had a
cavity in her lung and told her that she might not live for more

than two years, and that in any case she would have to undergo a serious operation. Realizing that tuberculosis was the family weakness, she felt that she had received a death sentence. When she came out of the consulting room she wondered what she ought to do next; she decided to go and have a large and expensive meal.

> The specialist wasn't *very* amusing [she wrote to a friend]. He says I have consumption in one lung, and wants to operate, which means going about on one lung for evermore. That doesn't seem to me to be much catch, especially as it seems to me not to be 'healing', as the other might go and then I should be in the soup. It's rather a mess up, isn't it? I don't feel I see the way through just yet. I must say I am a bit scared, but am trying to keep smiling.

She was in touch at this time with the Rev. John Maillard and derived much help from his belief in the power of faith to heal sickness and from his prayers. She found it difficult to make up her mind about going into hospital. Arrangements had been made and she was on her way there when something came to her in the train; she alighted at the next station and never went to the hospital.

She had a firm faith that God did not want a sick body and that, if He did not want that, it was not for her to allow herself to be sick. She became convinced that He still had work for her to do. The confidence grew that she would regain her health. She said in one of her talks in later years:

> Faith is not an easy thing to come by. You are fortunate if you have been ill enough to think that only faith will save you. Then you have to have it. You have to have it, when your body is saying the opposite that it is in the thrall, not of 'more abundant life,' but of sick life. You can gull yourself about the soul, not the body. You have to reiterate to yourself, and allow your imagination to dwell on it, that God is with *life* and that sickness is the enemy; that God is stronger than the enemy and He has looked on you, His creation, and said 'it is very good.' You have to know that it is His will that you have a perfect body as He made it to be. You may fail and fail but you may not go back on that faith.

It seemed clear that she ought to go to Switzerland, and her friends provided funds to enable her to spend the winter there. A letter written on the eve of her starting concludes with these words (her italics): '*I am happy. I want* to stand up tall and straight and worship like the larches do. I am a frightful pagan about just happiness. *Aren't things lovely?*'

She went to a sanatorium at Montana, and there met Miss Ruth Montgomery, who became one of her closest friends for the remainder of her life. Miss Montgomery writes:

> When in a sanatorium at Montana one was told with hushed voice that a missionary from Africa had arrived, one's thoughts at once rushed to a lady who might try to convert one. On the contrary, on being introduced to Miss Allshorn a sudden light broke into one's life—a gay, joy-loving person. A new interpretation of a missionary had arrived full of life and energy. The lady in question was subsequently asked to visit a young man from Africa, a government servant. He was in a critical condition, very shy and retiring, and somewhat loth to be visited by a missionary, and a woman at that. It was not long, however, before Florence became a daily visitor, and a very welcome one.

A few extracts from letters written from Montana will show how she reacted to this new experience.

> I'll tell you truly! At first it was worse or as bad as I had pictured a sanatorium would be. It *smelt* and looked like a hospital, and they put me in a room on the second floor next to a girl who coughed all night. And on Christmas Day the services really made me frantic, things were so sad you felt, people so anxious about their daughter or son or wife or someone, you just felt it was a *crying* thing all the time. I can't explain. But today I went to the manager and said I wasn't a bed patient and couldn't I move up higher, and he has given me a lovely double room, to the front with that heavenly view. It's so big I can prance about in it. I do love a big room. It's right up at the top, no smell and no coughs and I can sit and lie by the window and get possession of my soul again. I wish your soul didn't fly away so quickly when it gets out of one set of circumstances into another. I expect yours doesn't.

I haven't seen these mountains in the sunlight but I have in the moonlight and when you see them and they hit up against the thought of what is going on in those two bottom floors, it makes you *sure* that it isn't meant to be. Perhaps if mountains open glorious doors to God, He in His pity stoops and shows illness how to open equally glorious doors to Him; only I don't think they were what He meant, and *how can* He bear it all?

If I were rich I would spend all my money on a home where people like the boy who went yesterday could come when sanatoriums turn them out, and I would run it on faith healing lines and have people, doctors and nurses, who were trying hard for more faith, to help me run it. Wouldn't it be a gorgeous thing to do?

This morning I got a queer little conviction that somehow they (i.e. some of the patients) were going to be all right. Love felt awfully near and it is a kind of 'do a bit and then pass on' because you *can* only do *such* a bit, and God and Christ and Love are absolutely the same thing. They come in where you fail. Just like I felt about Iganga, only more intense because it is so dreadful leaving people to face a *year* in bed with no one but busy nurses flying in and getting you done as quick as they can.

Florence returned to England largely cured. She was advised to take another year of rest and was given permission to spend it more or less as she liked. It proved to be one of the most fascinating years of her life. An enterprising woman had started a new venture in Storrington at the foot of the South Downs. She had bought a piece of land and let any down-and-out, a struggling artist, an ex-convict, anyone in fact in need build a hut and live there. She lived there herself with her husband and had gathered a strangely assorted collection of people around her. Florence occupied one of these huts for a year. She loved her one-roomed home and meeting these odd people. She had stimulating talks with people of all kinds, many of whom questioned her religious views. She threw herself into the life of the community, walked on the Downs barefooted, acted in plays and for a year enjoyed a care-free, bohemian existence. The story can best be told in the words of the owner of the 'Sanctuary'.

I saw her first about twenty-five years ago, when she came to my Sanctuary in the hope of renting a studio for a while; a tall, slim, tweed-suited woman with a couple of dogs at her heels. 'Huntin', ridin' and fishin',' we said as she came towards us; breeding and niceness and all that, but we shall have little in common. We had not reckoned with the warmth of her smile, the deep sincerity and eagerness which gave her a kind of radiance, and those twinkling, wondering eyes. Within minutes we were finding her enchanting. Within days she had settled among, and won the affection of, a curious little community of some forty people (who were here because they *wished* to be here, never because they had been invited, vetted or chosen) who varied in colour, culture and creed. There were scoffers and clingers and I was very fond of them all. But, looking back, I often think how spiritually lonely I must have been till Florence came.

No one knew better than Florence the satisfaction of un-stinted service and the humility it implies. A guest of mine when she joined us was an atheist, and egoist, a communist and an extremely disintegrating, aggressive young man. Florence was a sick woman then, invalided back from Switzerland and actually convalescing here, with us. By chance my atheist learnt that she was a missionary.

'What?' he scoffed, 'an intelligent woman like that? It's the funniest thing I've heard in years.'

And, hooting with sadistic mirth, he set off for her studio, all set to 'shatter her illusions'.

'If you do anything to hurt Florence,' I called after him.

'Hurt? It's what Christians ask for,' he jeered. 'You with your crucified Christ.'

I never doubted the strength of her spirit. But she was several years my senior and after exacting work and her illness in need of peace and quiet. After an hour or so I went along anxiously. They were both of them laughing their heads off. It afterwards transpired that Paul, very soon wearying of attempting to shake so firm a faith, had concentrated on trying to shock her. He had started with the assumption that what she lacked was a lover and ended by showing her some indecent photographs. A not very pleasant person, but:

'I like him so much,' she said afterwards. 'He is funny and so un-grown-up. Like a little boy undoing vital buttons in public and quite expecting us to be startled to death.'

Paul was contemplating leaving the very pretty and devoted unmarried mother of his child. Florence sensed it, I think. One day she suggested he should take his Sally on the Downs; 'Oh Paul, she's so lovely.'

'Why yes, of course; I'm choosey; most certainly she is that.'

'Then tell her so, up there on the hills. She adores you. She would like that.'

'Romantic, aren't you? And what, pray, do we do with the brat?'

'I'll have him. I'd love to. Leave him with me.'

'All right, Christian,' he said suddenly. 'I darned well will.'

A little later he dumped the screaming baby, a bundle of nappies and a bottle, on her bed. Late that night they fetched an immaculate, sleeping child. Sally was tearful; it was not fair to Florence, she said. But 'Christian' had taken it in her stride, declared it was fun and, indeed, after that she had the infant for a day a week while Paul and Sally rediscovered each other—and *stayed together*—and Florence, despite the celibacy with which he constantly taunted her, taught Sally a thing or two concerning mothercraft. Hence the baby which had strained their nerves to breaking point became quite a contented child.

Florence, playing the piano for our country dancing round a camp fire, directing our dramatics, teaching us leather-craft, baking bread for my sick gipsies, bathing their grubby babies, joining in our discussions and our prayers. Florence, doing anything and everything that needed doing and always *doing it well*. How she loathed slovenliness and slackness. She was tremendously stimulating; she enjoyed everything and everyone (especially if 'difficult') and she set her standards sky high.

Florence came to gain from our Storrington Sanctuary. She stayed to give, as few have it in them to give. And what tremendous *fun* she was! She was always my ally in thoroughly shocking the hypocritically pious and the smug; a pleasure in which we indulged frequently and hilariously, like a couple of kids. We loved her for her warm humanity, her wide and sane perspective, her joyous *affirmation*, her courage, her enlightened tenderness; for the greatness of her heart and the quality of her mind.

Florence's own account of her experience at Storrington is given in the following extracts from her letters:

I wish I could really explain this place to you. I want you to *see* it in your mind. It is a colony of about thirty people, mostly very ordinary and quiet people, four nurses who are worn out nursing; a little woman with a husband invalided with shell-shock; mostly people who have been rather bashed about with life like that. We just try to be quite humble and friendly with them, and give them a warm, simple happy time here. Our huts are always ready for them to drop in and talk over any-thing or just to come without talking. It *is* what tired, muddled people, wrong people want more than anything. Time and this lovely country and friends can do such a lot.

But what is so mystifying to me is that the most loathsome gossip goes on in Storrington and it is worst among the church people. If we called ourselves a rescue or penitentiary centre they would be quite pleased with us, but just because we want to do it through the way we think Christ worked—friendship, they are dead against us and, whenever anything happens, they rise up and spread the most exaggerated stories about it all. I do want someone to put me in love with the Church again.

Well, here I am ensconced in my hut. I adore it and this simple life is quite the best kind of all. All the same I am fairly addled about my own situation. I do love mankind but at the same time I do realise that my love is rather acquiescent in mankind as it is. It's too tolerant, too broad. I suppose we are many of us re-acting from the intolerance there has been, but all the same I have a feeling that those who did renounce and deny themselves and were intolerant of any other way of doing things, even if they taught a very narrow way of looking at things, were much more nearly right than I am.

And when this winter is over, I am going to C.M.S. to see what they are going to do with me, and although I could much more easily work abroad, feeling as I do, than in the Church at home, I don't see at all a clear way. I don't *want* to work under committees or societies. I want to be free to experiment in things.

I love this life here, there's plenty to keep you going and not any waste of you at all. I have seen such lots of bits of life I had never known before, and it has made me feel that, if I did take up any job of the kind I have always done, I would want to go as a sweeper in one of the big music halls, or go and work in a factory or something, because I don't want to be outside. I want to be one of them and just do things through really being friends. I can't explain in a letter, but such hundreds of people aren't in touch with anything lovely at all, and it's those people I want to get at and show them a bit of what I see.

The following letter also appears to have been written at this time. Florence had the bad habit of not dating her letters. She sometimes gave the day of the week, occasionally the month. But she seldom gave the year (the letters from Uganda are an exception), and one has to depend on internal evidence, where this is available, or on the memory of her friends, to know to what period of her life a particular letter relates.

You say I have changed. I have, that's true. I am not learned, but I am always swinging forward about something, I think. Well—let me tell you. If you are not altering, you are slipping back—imperceptibly, perhaps. You will meet lots of women becoming a tiny bit more uninteresting, drabber, and duller. Now for the tonic. You have got to move, and how you are to do it with crowds of people round you I don't know. It kills the creative force in you always doing exactly what other people do. And the creative force is the thing in you that makes you grow. You need not have a brain or be a social success; you need to be very simple, very sure that all your life is founded on sincere things. I do think that not to *see* bigness all the time, so that you grow bigger, is so sad. I have met one big person lately who isn't a Christian, though her belief in God is bigger than anything we could ever attain to, I mean the conception she has. And it's what I want so in people. I want some one to sweep me out and up into something huge and wide.

When Florence wrote about bigness she was not thinking of something that would fill a large place in the public eye. What she coveted was largeness of heart and mind. There was, in fact, waiting for her a work which, though it did not lie in the sphere of public action, was so directly related to the real values of human life that she could in it 'see bigness all the time,' and grow continually in stature through seeing it.

IV

TRAINING MISSIONARIES

IN 1928 FLORENCE ALLSHORN received an urgent invitation from the Church Missionary Society to fill a temporary gap by becoming warden of St Andrew's Hostel, one of the two training colleges for women missionaries belonging to the Society.

She had no idea how a missionary college should be conducted. She had never been at one herself. She lacked the normal academic qualifications for such a post. But she felt that the Society had been very kind to her during her illness and that, if she was really needed, she must be ready to help. She was conscious also that her experience in Uganda had taught her something that missionaries needed to learn. She was aware that the situation which she had encountered there was not unique. She knew that women were going out to the mission field with high ideals but with too little understanding how to relate these to ordinary living. She had seen women break down under the stress of isolation, or—what she always felt to be an even worse evil—growing hard and bitter and becoming reconciled to a situation in which enmity between missionaries was a denial of all that they preached. If God was calling her to pass on to others what she had learned in the hard school of experience, it was her duty to obey. She often would say laughingly that she had not any qualifications for being head of a training college, the only subjects she knew anything about being domestic science and personal relations, though she did know a little about them. Into what a wealth of understanding and wisdom they were for Florence Allshorn the gateway, this and the following chapter will show.

The transition from the Sanctuary at Storrington to St

Andrew's was from a world of unconventionality and bohemian-
ism to one of strict propriety and a somewhat narrow orthodoxy.
The astonishing thing about Florence was that she was at home
and happy and the same whole and entirely genuine person in
both.

She had her difficulties in the early years with the authorities
of the Church Missionary Society. Her abounding vitality would
not fit into any of the moulds in which people of narrower vision
and lesser reach sought to comprehend life.

She had to face the resistance [writes one of the secretaries of the
society] of many who were puzzled and alarmed by her failure
to conform to any conventional pattern of belief and practice.
But what irritated or alarmed people at one moment, reassured
them at the next. I was immensely tickled to watch those who
were on the point of denouncing some heresy in her teaching
taken aback by discovering that she was preaching one of their
pet shibboleths with a flame of earnestness and sincerity which
outshone their own.

It was several years before suspicions were allayed. Perhaps
they were never entirely laid to rest. But in the end Florence won
the confidence of even the conservative element in the Society,
as it became clear that she belonged to no party and presented to
all a challenge in her devotion to truth and fearless living. The
confidence was shown six years later when in 1934 the two
colleges of St Andrew's Hostel and Kennaway Hall for the training of women missionaries were amalgamated and Florence
Allshorn was appointed principal of the combined institution.
The trust reposed in her found warm expression in the minutes
that were passed by the Executive Committee on her retirement
from the work of training in 1941 and on the occasion of her
death. In the latter minute it is said that 'her outlook and teaching
have left an impress upon the life of the Society as a whole which
will be enduring in its effects.'

Except for a house-mother and the help of visiting lecturers
Florence was single-handed in the job she had undertaken. Her
feeling about it is expressed in letters written at the time:

It's the most marvellous job really. As usual I do think I am one of the most fortunate people in the world because it's such a chance to do something. I've got a real passion for quality in souls, and somehow I seem to be two people, one of which God can use in a creative way that is really changing people so that they are all developing some positive thing in themselves that is quite different in each one. And the other 'me' is the most awful futile thing that ever breathed, and there isn't a single one of them that is not 'up on me'.

I wonder how long it will take me to learn this job. I have got to learn to disentangle the bad bits so that the good bits have room to grow, to smash fetters without smashing the hands they imprison (only souls are so much more delicate than hands) and to set feet in a true direction. We are too 'Protestant' here to have much use for the word beauty, but I can see beautiful things getting smothered in so many of them, mostly too not by actual sin, but by unreal Christianity and an easy self-satisfaction. Well at the bottom of each one of them there is a spark of divine discontent and I'll be the bellows to blow it into such a flame that they will be safe for ever—oh, if I could!

Florence slipped unobtrusively into her task. At first she was viewed with a certain suspicion by students who had a conservative outlook. But she quickly won the confidence of most. The new measures which she introduced met with growing appreciation. She made changes in the diet with a view to strengthening the students for years of strenuous service abroad. Believing, as she did, in the importance of culture and art as a background to the spiritual life, she set herself to develop the cultural life of the college. She did all she could to beautify the house. Her own taste in dress set an example in the matter of clothes. To change for supper was *de rigueur*. She increased the number of books of poetry and about art in the library. She invited people with cultural interests to the house. She read poetry aloud, took her students to the art galleries, and fostered an interest in music.

She became the friend of the students, sharing as fully as possible in all their life. She made them feel that she was deeply interested in their future, apart from their training. She entered into their frolics, keeping St Patrick's Day with the Irish, trundling hoops round Clissold Park for a dare, laughing the heartiest at a freshers' social or sleeping out with the students in the summer garden. At Sunday teas, when honey sandwiches were the order of the day, the students would sit on the floor in her room and listen to the letters from former students now abroad as missionaries. The intercession service for them every Sunday morning in chapel was the focussing point of prayer for the week.

Her capacity for enjoyment was infectious. She could enjoy the simplest things with the most complete delight, and could forget all about her work very rapidly. Her irrepressible sense of humour made many things possible that would have been impossible to anyone who did not possess it. It was one of the things that made her contacts with people easy. She could approach the most difficult problems with so light a touch that people were scarcely aware that she was dealing with them. To begin with, she was very shy, but she always broke through her shyness to help other people and never allowed it to hinder her from fulfilling her task. As the years passed her natural shyness seemed to fall away from her and an inner sureness emerged.

The way in which she was able, in spite of her previous ill-health, to sustain a heavy college programme, with constant personal interviews and personal demands on her of all kinds, often seemed a miracle. She was enabled to fight her battle with ill-health by her unfaltering belief in the healing power of Christ. When she was overtired and overstrained, she would go to her own room and stay in bed for a day or two until she could re-grasp the reality of His healing. Sometimes her vitality would return quite suddenly, and sometimes it would take longer, but again and again, when it was thought that she was going to break down, she would re-appear among her students looking rested and refreshed and full of new ideas.

The task to which Florence directed all her energies was to discover and release in each of her students the capacities which she believed to exist in everyone.

I wonder why there are so many defeated women of forty. That's a secret I have got to learn more of. They must all have

D

been full of possibilities once like these students. What happens? If we could find out what happens we could prevent these youngsters following the same road.

I can't bear the idea of these young possibilities alongside the mediocre, tamed thing life becomes for so many. I believe it is fundamentally the root evils that remain unconquered that rob the religious person as well as the irreligious of their radiancy and gaiety, stop growth and blind them in the end to everything that moves Godward. You can't *afford* defeat anywhere in you. I must learn to find the secret in them, for them.

Florence's approach to students was that of the artist rather than the teacher. She did not think of herself as a mature person imparting some knowledge, insight or skill to someone less mature, but worked rather with a picture of what the person she was dealing with might become. She assumed that the other also desired to achieve that perfection, so that both were working together to attain to something outside and greater than themselves. 'Once you realize that everything—including man—has a perfection, then the perfection of each student must be desired and sought. I must be disinterested there, and take as much joy in my work for each one as a poet takes in writing a poem.'

I do feel Protestantism works too much on a sub-conscious feeling of suspicion—possibly because it is so concerned, sincerely concerned, with sin—that it loses the vision of the lovely thing a human soul really is, a thing trembling with hope because *somewhere*—stifled to death almost but somewhere— it has a knowledge that it could become a son of God. It gets pressed down and down under these 'self' things and no one is merciful enough to go down and get it out from underneath. But you know even in the most trying and 'bad' person, there is a tiny look or a movement of the lips or head which *shows* this wistful goodness. I am always seeing it and whenever I do I long to give it its freedom.

In reply to a suggestion that she should write a book on her ideas of training she wrote:

I think my ideas aren't any good unless you start by really caring for the perfection of people—really seeing the beauty of a soul. Do I sound priggish? I am trying to say something. If people tried my way without seeing that, they'd do it wrong and make an awful mess of it. I think I see them that way not because I am better than other people, but because I have got an artistic sense well related all round, not just in art as such. I can't leave people at 'she's such a nice woman, but—'. It's the 'best' I want to help them to get at.

And *seeing*—that's so rare and so important and people go blind because they won't obey the next step. They play about with the 'but', then escape by saying 'we're only human' or 'well, after all we can't be perfect'. It's finding your way out of the vague easy going life that's the life of disciplined endeavour, only the disciplined endeavour isn't *not* doing things, it's going through and beyond things.

Part of my training has been rotten, but one part is different from the ordinary outlook of principals of training colleges, and I'd like to get it down. I haven't given the students any knowledge, because I haven't got any, but I've taught them to think and see. It has been a very muddled affair because I've had no one to help me, but we got somewhere. I believe our great trouble is that we won't stir up courage to look at *failure*.

She always looked on the two great commandments as the foundation of everything she was attempting to do, and thought much about their relation to one another.

We have been seeing some of the Little Plays of St Francis. He gave me some big things. The way he was so certain that, if a thing was God's will, it would happen, and where he had to be the instrument, he was quite happy and peaceful about it. And then his caring—such a hotch-potch of people he had, pious ones, quarrelsome ones, stupid ones, and he *delighted* in them all. He was so large and gentle and terribly wise with them. And, of course, because of his right attitude he was a happy man. It *is* those two attitudes that are the two Commandments worked out in everyday life.

There is all the difference in the world between religious people and Christ-like people. You can be religious and yet somehow keep self as the largest thing, because being consciously unselfish isn't necessarily selflessness at all. But to be able to delight in God and others to such an extent that 'I want' goes right out *is* the heart of it.

I feel I have worked hard on that second commandment these three years because I had that reaction from the lovelessness abroad, and I have made these people *see* that thing. But I had been missing the first too much and I have been getting back to it this last term, not letting go the second, and I am more solidly happy than I have ever been. It takes such ages getting straightened out—with me longer than anyone in the world, I think.

In her dealing with her students she could be very drastic in diagnosis, but for most people it was easier to take the truth from her than from any other source, because she never once lost sight of the student as God wanted her to be. There was never any questioning of her motives in telling people the truth about themselves. The richer the possibilities that she saw in a student, the more drastic she would be about the weaknesses—provided that she knew that the student could stand it. She had a sure instinct which enabled her to know when people could stand things and when they couldn't. Because all were aware of the truth of her intention and knew that she wanted the very best for them, she was able to say things that they could at that time have taken from no one else. 'There's so much weak and unreal surface pleasantness about', she writes in a letter. 'I can go on at that level with a student for months. Then something happens and she's miserable, and because she's knocked out of her shallow undisturbedness she's so much more lovable suddenly. Oh yes! anything that *bangs* you into *something*. Not these niggardly little troubles of relationships and one's own peevishness.'

Florence realized that the starting-point in training is always where a person *is*, and she was constantly impressing this on her colleagues.

It will be very difficult for her to understand you and for you to understand her. You will have to get where she is and take her on from there and that takes time. Don't try to make her toe right up to what you see, because she can't.

She becomes incoherent because you don't find her and begin there; you try to pull her up to what you see. It's the danger of all us single-minded fanatics, because that is what we do become if we can't get where the other person is.'

Training was always looked upon by Florence as a reciprocal process. She had a remarkable capacity for learning from other people, even from those who were much less mature than herself. She once said that no student had passed through her hands who had not taught her something.

One of the things that stands out very clearly, as I look back [writes a colleague who was with her on the staff at Kennaway Hall for four years] is that, in spite of, or perhaps because of, her adventurous and ever-moving spirit, she was a very easy person to live and work with. I think this was because of her infinite patience. I have never met anyone who had so great a passion for perfection together with such loving patience with the imperfections in us all. Of course she made mistakes, and she would be the first to laugh at us if we drew too glowing a picture. She often said that in these early years she had made many mistakes with people. Sometimes she expected too much of them, sometimes she took them at their face value and did not see the weakness beneath. Sometimes she would try to push them further than they could go.

No account of Florence's time at St Andrew's Hostel and Kennaway Hall would be complete without a reference to the long holidays which educational work allows, and which Florence particularly enjoyed. She would often have one of her students with her. One who became later a close friend recalls her first experience of a shared holiday.

I was asked [she writes] to a small cottage that she had rented for the Christmas holidays, with frost and full moon and everything clean and exciting. We did nothing but walk together and sew and cook our meals, but being with her all day was the most stimulating of all tonics—a never-to-be-forgotten time.

Florence was later given a small bungalow built on the ledge of the cliffs—it has since fallen over them—near Mundesley in

Norfolk. She spent many care-free and happy holidays there. Breakfast was more often than not taken outside in the sunshine on the edge of the cliff, and after it one could run down a steep path straight into the sea and bathe. Florence took a special delight in foreign travel, and one of her greatest joys was to pay a visit to the Continent with one of her friends.

As the story of St Julian's will show, she had a constant urge to reach out to larger things. She had never looked on Kennaway Hall as a suitable centre, and in 1938 she initiated and successfully carried out a move to Foxbury in Chislehurst—a charming house with accommodation for forty students in eight acres of lovely grounds. She had been able at last to collect the staff she had always wanted. But she had been there for only three terms when the war came. The Church Missionary Society decided to close the college and make Foxbury the temporary headquarters of the Society during the war. After ten years of much difficulty in getting people to adopt her ideas and follow her lead, and acquiring at last what seemed to her the ideal place for training, all was swept away in a night. But she did not mind. She loved building more than carrying on. She said of herself that she was acquisitive, not possessive.

A month later the Church Missionary Society asked her to take a reduced number of students to Selly Oak, where accommodation was provided at Carey Hall. She was there for a year. During that period her thoughts began to turn in a fresh direction. She realized that she was tired, and the conviction grew on her that the time had come to give up the principalship of the training college. Towards the end of the year she decided to resign, and offered to carry on for one more term. As there had been no serious bombing it was decided to reopen Foxbury as a training college, but the staff and students had no sooner settled in than the Battle of Britain began. Foxbury was in the zone of heavy bombing and the college was evacuated to Ridley Hall, Cambridge. When the term there ended at Christmas, Florence was free for a new adventure.

V

ESSENTIALS OF MISSIONARY
PREPARATION

IT USED to be said with a certain dry humour in the years
following the World Missionary Conference of 1910, when the
preparation of missionaries was a subject of active discussion in
missionary circles, that to give a missionary the full equipment
indispensable for his task, in theology, the theory and practice
of education, anthropology, sociology, the history, methods and
problems of missions, elementary medicine and hygiene and so
on, obviously required ten or twelve years of further training
after graduation. Not all Florence Allshorn's students were
graduates, and the usual length of time for which she had them
was for four terms, i.e. less than a year and a half. Training under
these circumstances was, like politics, 'the art of the possible.'

While the proportions varied a little from term to term, about
one-third of the students sent for training were teachers, some of
them graduates, one-third nurses and the remaining third women
without any professional qualification, while there were in
addition generally two or three doctors.

It was Florence's genius that in any problem with which she
had to deal she succeeded in fastening at once on the essentials and
in holding firmly to them. Her conception of what was essential
in the training of missionaries was highly original and profound.
The depth and richness of her thinking on this subject have not
yet found recognition outside the limited circle which she directly
influenced. Her ideas go to the roots of the problem of training
for the Christian ministry and for all forms of Christian work.

They deserve the attention of those concerned with such training in all countries.

But to understand Florence Allshorn's contribution to this important subject, it is necessary to distinguish between her fundamental thought and the practical expression of it which was forced on her by circumstances. It was her habit to concentrate all her energies on the problem she was called to deal with, and not to indulge in general reflections. But this should not be allowed to obscure the fact that in her handling of the specific task allotted to her there are implicit principles capable of the widest application.

One of the best statements of what Florence Allshorn conceived to be essential and primary in the training of missionaries is contained in an article on 'The Corporate Life of a Mission Station,' which she contributed to the *International Review of Missions* in 1934. She recorded later that she had had letters of appreciation of the article from all the leading missionary societies in Great Britain and from some in other countries but that, so far as she could see, it had brought about no changes in existing practice. A fairly full quotation from this article will perhaps be the best introduction to the ideas which governed Florence Allshorn's approach to her task.

> There is a queer dark core of shame that undoubtedly lies rankling in our hearts when we think of our human relationships in the missions. We dare not leave them as they are, and sometimes it seems to me that, if we do not go down deeper into that second commandment of Jesus Christ, the spiritual life in us will peter out altogether. If the whole realm of missionary human relationships is to be left in the nebulous and frustrate state in which it now is, our preaching of any message of salvation will be almost in vain. It is in relation to this that I want to show the difficulties which exist for the modern woman recruit going out for the first time, while recognizing as fairly as I can the bewilderment with which the pre-war mind must regard the strange mixture of extreme capability and ardent immaturity which is the modern young woman of to-day.
>
> If Christ cannot save me from those things that jar on my fellow-missionary, then I have but a thin message of salvation; and if I cannot help my English sister to get through certain

selfish attitudes which create unhappiness for myself or any one else, how can I say that I have come to help my African or Indian sister to get through hers?

In creating and building up any work which is to be a balanced and perfect whole we need a whole mind working on it. No single mind is a whole mind. Minds can be roughly divided into three types. First, there are those rare minds, not much in evidence in this day of technical and mechanistic thought and generally found in not too robust bodies, which have the gift of initiative and creative insight. Missionaries with these minds are invaluable to any group of builders. They trouble the waters of our so-easily-fixed habits, urge us to escape into a larger world, and do it by hurling at us a further challenge. Then there are the intellectual minds, which can be the necessary tools for the practical application of the fruits of insight. And lastly, there are the repetitive minds which carry out the scheme.

I am well aware that you cannot arbitrarily cut people into those three categories, but I say that all the capacities are necessary. And I say it because I want to put in a plea for an intelligent recognition of a young missionary's individual capacity and for a chance to be given her to develop it to the best.

The first type of mind is the most difficult—a trouble to the owner herself and everyone else while she is young. Under stress of circumstances she can only become either more creative or neurotic; there is no middle way. Being eager and sensitive, a restive spirit against prison bars, she is more liable to nervous strain than the more temperate type. It takes her longer to adjust to life. To follow its truth her mind has to deepen and she is for a time self-centred, not from choice but from necessity. She easily acquires an inferiority complex which undermines self-confidence and if she hits her idealistic head too long on monotonous and (to her) almost valueless routine, the positiveness of her eager initiative is replaced by the negativeness of a more or less submissive resignation; she either breaks down or tames down, and the latter is the greater and more frequent tragedy. Such a mind is an unmitigated nuisance to an older woman who wants it 'for the job'; but for one who has enough sensitive intelligence to see the truth, surely there is a real delight in helping to develop its wings.

We all stand in front of a situation in which the amount of
work we have to get through in school or hospital seems sometimes the only thing that fills the horizon. People with these
minds, if we will only give them their chance, are those who
may lead us out of the impasse. They will not find a 'solution'
for the 'problem'. (Those two words, as L.P. Jacks reminds us,
are not mentioned in the Bible at all.) They will do more than
solve a problem, they will lead us out to face a further challenge.
We desperately need creative, spiritual thinkers, but we too often
turn them into neurotics and then say what a nuisance they are.

Above all others, such people need their time of silence and
quiet. To rob them is to do them untold harm physically,
mentally and spiritually.

With regard to the second type of mind, the intellectual,
we have two sorts, the strong and the weaker. In the strong
there is an urgent desire for knowledge which will not be let,
whatever the circumstances. But there are dozens of young
missionaries who with a little encouragement and chance would
not have let their mental powers go to such waste as is actually
the case. The same cry of 'no time' robs them of this birthright
too. They come back keen on 'the job' but with their minds
already in the rut of 'the job' and more or less satisfied that it
should be so.

The repetitive type of mind is beloved of the overworked
senior, and things being as they are who can wonder? But there
is danger for people with this type of mind too, unless the
senior is awake to it. You can work to a vision, or you can pass
your time simply reacting to the needs of the moment. It
makes a wide and fateful difference which you do, and this
type of woman needs help in keeping some kind of vision
before herself.

The failures amongst missionaries are those who have lost
the forward impulse, the life of the Spirit, because they have
never got through their own spiritual, personal and social
problems. This may be due either to the fact that they were the
wrong kind to send out—people whose spiritual life was unreal—or because they have been caught in the cog of the
mechanical routine of too much work, and have become
exhausted and unable to deal with their problems. Failing to
find success in their spiritual and mental life they are seeking it
by putting almost all their vitality into 'the job'.

But womanhood may not do that; womanhood means more than a bright vision of success in 'a job'; it means patience and longsuffering and the deepening of gentlenesses; it means going down into deep places. Can success be taught to any young colleague by women who have grown old and sterile in spirit, who have not themselves had the help or the courage to face and acknowledge the things that are important and the things that are not?

We must see that failure is not repeated. We have made one great mistake in our training. We have spent much time in educating the girl in her spiritual life and preparing her for her work, but her emotional life we have left largely to take care of itself; and it is in the emotional life—this queer hinterland which is in all of us—that there huddle the anxieties, timidities, antagonisms, self-deceptions, inferiorities, revenge attacks, superiorities and withdrawals which somehow our spiritual life does not go deep enough to touch, where all the fighting and friction and the wreckage begin and end. If a woman fails to adjust her emotional life and goes on unconsciously working with a sense of failure there, then the one spot where she can find success is in 'the job'; but the almost inevitable result of a sense of failure in the inner life of a woman is an urgent desire for power. I believe that to be the chief reason why women missionaries—and indeed those at home, too, when they get into some position of authority—so often lose that integral quality of Christ-likeness, humility, and become so hard and dominating and so rabid about their work.

Success must find its home on the spiritual plane above all and first of all. If success in 'the job' comes first, then life is certain to be foiled of its home and its peace, and if a recruit cannot cope with the spiritual and mental tensions as well as the physical tensions of the mission station, and cannot get help from her senior, then unless she has an extraordinarily strong and stabilized character naturally, she too can only follow the same losing course. Only those women who have stabilized their own emotional lives can know what is happening to any life in the process of stabilization, and can show a clear way through. There would be hope if we at home and those abroad could get fired with the conviction that the present situation is not good enough, that there is a forward step of understanding and a deeper way of knowing, which hold the salvation for which we are looking. It is not that we are blaming people for failing; no one has a right to blame anyone but herself, but there is everything to learn and to understand, and the road to the new happiness in relationships is a road of far more intelligence, far more honesty, far more realism and far more freedom for people to find their own way to spiritual beauty than we have so far travelled.

Whatever the other qualifications needed, we must send out people who are growing into the kind of personality which will react, as to a living stimulus, to every possible condition. We must look for the signs of a conquering personality.

For most women candidates the training should be long enough to give time for self-understanding and for stabilizing emotional life on some kind of conquering basis. This is the most essential thing to learn and for some a year is far too short. When a recruit has become aware of something in herself which may mar her future, it is obviously not by seeing what is wrong that she is saved. Old habits of mind have to be replaced by new habits of thought and they are so obstinate that this takes time.

We shall have to realize that in building up the recruit the mental and emotional health is of even more importance than the health of the body. Few men, I think, can fully understand how much the emotional life of a woman plays in the matter of her health, and this is far more acute in tropical countries.

We are seeing with humbled eyes that only a loving super-personal Power can rescue us from the impasse, on the one hand of being overwhelmed by the impossibility of any situation, on the other, of becoming hardened to it. We see, too, a new valuation of a deeper kind of reality arising, based on the psychological understanding of human nature, which surely contains the germ of a better way of living together. It seems to me there is here the point at which advance must lie, a point where we penetrate a little more deeply into those two commandments of Jesus Christ, which, after all, are the laws of the Kingdom. We must be in agreement with those two commandments, or we are on the wrong road. They are the test of the right road.

This review of the missionary situation is an illustration of Florence's remarkable gift of penetrating at once to the heart of things. The essential thing in the fulfilment of the missionary task was that the Christian witness should be *real*. Her experience in Africa had made her see in a new way the inadequacy of conventional religion. She realized that much of her thinking, her Bible reading and, as she would often say, her hymn-singing had been unrelated to reality. She saw too that the relations between people were the test of real love of Jesus Christ. To that challenge she responded with her entire being. What she knew to be necessary for herself, she realized to be no less necessary for those whom she was training to be missionaries. 'All you can do for them', she wrote to a colleague, 'is to be a sign-post to something more real.'

Reality meant for Florence Allshorn a true and right relation to the two fundamental realities of human existence—God and neighbour. She always said that the time allowed for training was so short that there was time only for the essentials, and to her the essentials were the students' life with God and her capacity to live with her fellow-students.

The relation of the student to God was for Florence the fundamentally important thing, because out of that everything would grow, whereas if that relation was broken or weakened there would be no growth. She did not pry into the relation between another soul and God or try to lay clumsy hands upon it. She was content to stand ready to help, if her help was wanted, and she watched for the fruits of a student's relation to God in the community—in humility, in selflessness, in ability to get on with other people, in the power to overcome dislikes and to control emotions. How she understood the relation with God can best be expressed in her own words. She says in a memorandum about training:

However many complacent excuses we may make about 'not being perfect', we are called to be 'saints', and a saint is a person who has learned to be possessed by God with whose love she confronts enemy as well as friend. If this definite learning of the love of God in reality and truth does not in practice and act take first place in our training at home or abroad, what strength and clarity of direction have we in our training? St Catharine of Sienna (whose biography is on the library shelves of all our training colleges) *after seeing God* became one of the most famous and one of the most powerful women of her century, endlessly active, travelling, shaping the life of Christendom. Why do we not set our pattern towards her experience? Why start in them this endless activity before being sure that they have the 'seeing' in some degree tuned to reality? Why cut our pattern by the good kind pagan plus a little devotion to a religious ideal?

I know this does not sound kind nor even quite true, and few will find it acceptable enough to face. If they looked at the mediocre results of our Christianity they might be forced to do so. At any rate it is too near the truth; and it is the woman who is alert and alive to her own spiritual adventure who looking back on her own training days would say that herself. That every recruit has a true and effective spiritual life is taken too much for granted, and we have a queer belief that the Holy Spirit will do the job for us if we ask, occasionally in some little ardent way, and hundreds of times coldly. But the grace and power of the Holy Spirit, let us make no mistake about it, offered with its divine generosity as it is, is only half the story; to be able to accept it we must have learned from God how to purify the will, we must have learned the lesson of detachment from the self-will and its proprietorships. The one is given as the other is learned; therefore we do not want secular colleges with a religious bias, pushing in knowledge of theology, anthropology, Bible, etc., as if they were matters to be learned like maths. For the second stage of training at all events we want a religious house (with its connotation) for the training —not a religious house divorced from the world of sinners and worldly men, but a community of people struggling to become God-possessed, where they will find the world too as well as the deeper commitments of God.

For most people it is a very slow, long, arduous business, the business of being re-born, the endless day to day struggle to find God, to come nearer to God, to think and will more and more exclusively as He thinks and wills; and to be partners in Christ's redemptive work.

A true relation with God *must* in Florence's view issue in a genuine love for people. Obedience to the second commandment was always for her the test of obedience to the first. It seemed to her that the word 'love' was constantly being interpreted with a 'corrupt conscience.' Under the influence of the lassitude, dislike of control and shrinking from pain that were the aftermath of the first World War, 'the great, stern, austere command became watered down into the prevailing indulgent laxity. It came from the lips of people who had thrown aside discipline, and even righteous anger, and who were themselves victims of that most grotesque reaction to truth—self-expression.' People talked about love and wrote books about it, but they did not set themselves to study seriously what Jesus taught about it and the way in which He lived it. 'Few set themselves steadily to face the cost of learning it, with its divine indignations, its compassions, its wrath against those who by their self-expressionism harmed and hurt others.'

Those who learned to live in daily, growing, whole-hearted response to the two great realities of man's life, God and neighbour, became really free persons. They were delivered from self-centredness, from the complaining 'I want' and 'I feel', and given a new centre outside themselves.

Preoccupation with self was for Florence the one hateful, maiming, thwarting, deadly hindrance to the rich and joyous fulfilment of life. The thought recurs over and over again in her letters. The following extracts are examples.

It is only as we vow ourselves to obedience that we begin to see that we, as we are, can never enter this fresh, free, utterly lovely Kingdom of heavenly love. That takes us a long time because of the 'I' ingrained in every beat of our heart, every movement of our minds, every habit of our habitual days;—slowly, by determined will, we have to empty ourselves. When humility is there we start really following, but not before. It is the first obedience; to disobey the order to be humble turns us into Pharisees, hypocrites, and pious prigs.

I hope all goes well with you. It will when the 'I' is taken out. Not till then. When you really see that so deeply that you are acting a little on it, you wonder why on earth you clung to that little puffed-up being so long. The release and clearness of the joy is so different and the peace at the centre of you. I know that I shan't let you rest till you do.

All these lessons had to be learned in *practice*. To bring that about was the purpose of training. These were not the kind of lessons that could be taught in theory. Florence knew well that response to God and to the other person is something that can only be lived.

At the heart of the training lay training in the life of prayer and corporate, as well as private, Bible-study. These were redeemed from any tendency to pietism by the fact that the test of everything learned was always action.

Students had to be trained to 'feed on difficulties', a phrase of John R. Mott which Florence was fond of quoting.

> When some difficulty [she wrote to a colleague] is brought to us as members of the staff, our attitude should be, 'Well, here it is, what are you going to do about it?' rather than to try sympathetically to solve it for her. Relate it to some situation on the mission where she will probably be alone. Circumstances are their practice ground. Therefore welcome difficulties for the students in training. Help them to find their way through with the Saviour. Don't teach them to lean on you.

For practice in the all-important matter of personal relations the college community itself provided ample opportunities. 'Help the student to cope with the girl she dislikes. Put them at a job together, interpret them to each other. Don't let her off till she *knows how to refuse defeat.*'

The aim must be to help the student to commit herself to a life of *learning*. To succeed in that was to plant in her the capacity for continuous growth. If she learned the secret of responding freely and directly to God and to people, every fresh experience that life brought to her would make her a larger person. The student

> must show herself a learner, not only in academic matters, but in small things. The danger out there is that we have so much to pass over to others that it can keep us going for a long time, but if a girl has not the capacity for learning, she will not learn any more and will dry up, and she will not be open enough, nor eager enough to learn from Africans.

> What is it [she asked in later years] that prevents people from becoming effective leaders? Chiefly the fact that they *stop growing*. They try to face very complicated problems and tasks

at an immature level of the spiritual life—and give up, falling back on that most dolorous of all refuges, spiritual window-dressing.

Life for her was in an extraordinary degree a single whole. She could not therefore be content with what is so common —an academic training given in a devotional atmosphere. That was not enough 'to get the fundamental attitudes straight.'
Florence was fully aware of the demands which this kind of training makes on those who try to give it. They can give it only by *being* the kind of persons they want missionaries to be.

It all depends on the leader, the principal. If she is not herself knowing God, and knowing *that to know God* is the most important subject on the curriculum, knowing Him in its many ramifications of working out in will and deed, she will dilute every standard in some degree to a pitiful little psychological insight and a half-sad, half-cynical hoping for the best. And mediocrity will still sag the witness at home and abroad, taming the burning fire of the Holy Spirit.

The things that have been described were in Florence Allshorn's view the essentials of missionary training. If they were allowed to dominate, everything else could find its proper place in that framework.
Doctrine must occupy the central place in the curriculum. It belonged to Florence's realism that there was no use in people going out to be missionaries unless they knew what they were going to teach. She did all in her power to give to the students, so far as was possible in the time at her disposal, a good grounding in Christian doctrine, and in particular in the Bible itself. But she held equally firmly to the conviction that religious truth is assimilated only in so far as it is lived. She was never content with a merely intellectual grasp of Christian doctrine; she watched eagerly for its translation into life. Doctrine, she held, must have

the place of supreme importance in the training of missionary students—a place of such supreme importance that it must not be separated from the whole of the programme. Its position in
E

this training is that it is related directly to the total experience of training of each person. The truths we know and teach must 'be proved upon our pulses.' They must find root in the life of every day.

Florence did not undervalue academic studies. She was keenly alive to their importance for the student. She constantly lamented any curtailing of the lecture syllabus. She also attached high importance to practical experience gained in the running of girls' clubs and similar social activities. But she steadily set herself to keep first things first. She often discussed the possibility of students taking examinations in their training, but always came back to the point that, once they started working for examinations, the real drive might go into that rather than into their spiritual life and growth. This was not because she did not appreciate the value of good qualifications—she rated them highly, but because, as she often said, 'it is no good a woman having a first-class degree if she can't live with her fellow missionaries.'

While God and people were for Florence the fundamental realities, she was not indifferent to the world of nature and the wider life of society. She loved it passionately because it was God's world. All that went on in it was of interest to her. History, comparative religion, the theory and practice of education, psychology, anthropology, moral hygiene, domestic subjects, children's clinics for ante-natal and after care and practical nursing had their place in the curriculum or were pursued in classes outside. What could be learned of these subjects in the time available was in most cases a mere smattering. But it was given in a way to open the eyes of the student to what might be learned from these various branches of knowledge so that she could according to her bent pursue her studies while she was at work, or take a special course when she came on furlough.

Florence always attached a high importance to questions of health.

A great deal can be done [she writes] in the training period to get at small habitual ailments. The most successful experiment we put into practice was to have a woman doctor (young) who had been abroad, to come and visit the College for a day and a night. She gave them short talks on minor and common ailments, and stayed for the rest of the day to see each student privately. All kinds of minor ailments came out which would add to the weight of the struggle abroad—things like small recurring headaches, indigestion, piles, feet ailments, etc. She came at the beginning of each term, gave advice, and visited again towards the end to see what had been done. Women tend to cover up minor ailments, but aching feet due to a weak instep can be the last straw for those who have to stand on them in a tropical climate most of the day.

It was not for nothing that domestic science was Florence's second specialism besides personal relations. It helped her to keep a true balance.

I *know* our malaise is [she writes] that the so-called spiritual is devoured by the material. That is why I love to be in the kitchen. The spiritual isn't there somehow, unless you are working with your own hands and mind at a *standard*, together, a delight. There's a perfect satiety of ideas, but it's all 'we ought, we must, we shall'. Where is it to be worked out except in groups doing actual so-called material tasks together, it doesn't matter how small and hum-drum. I feel as if I were so young and ignorant before the integrated thing life could be —and I have a small revulsion from books at the moment. All the time we are writing and reading books God is *doing* it. The only thing is to go and serve, with body, soul and spirit, the integrated whole.

To serve, with body, soul and spirit, an integrated whole—that was Florence Allshorn.

VI

TOWARDS ST JULIAN'S

FLORENCE had come to the conclusion that the preliminary training of missionaries, the first term of service and a period of further training during the first furlough was a stage in a missionary's life which ought to be envisaged as a single whole, and had persuaded the Church Missionary Society of the rightness of this view.

Experience had shown her the limitations of what could be achieved in the initial period of training. 'You really cannot do much in the initial training', she wrote to a colleague. 'They have not come to the end of themselves, you can only gently try to make them more real.' There was much also that could better be learnt—perhaps could only be learnt—after experience had been gained of actual work in the mission-field. Most important of all was the need to face uncompromisingly the spiritual failing which the period of service overseas had revealed. Some of the things that were in Florence's mind find expression in the following extracts from a memorandum she wrote about this time.

In the light of my experience of dealing for over ten years with young missionaries coming back for their first furlough, I think they fall perhaps into four categories.

(1) People who seem satisfied with their life and their service and are simply getting down to making themselves fitted to do that job better.

(2) Those who feel they did a pretty good spiritual thing but might have done better.

(3) Those who have found in themselves some hard rooted emotional problem which has ruined the purpose and witness of their missionary work—far more common than we are inclined to think.

(4) People who went out in the first place on a very big spiritual adventure. They were up against principalities and powers—the Devil did not like these people. They were rather immature in Christ and found they could not cope—came home feeling very unsuccessful Christians.

At any rate people would fit somewhere roughly into those four groups. I think the people who are dissatisfied, knowing some kind of failure in their time abroad are the most hopeful. Someone wrote once: 'Best men are long in making; he that soon sparkles and flourishes as soon is gone.'

It is better to feel a failure over tackling a big thing than to feel a success over tackling a less—it is better to have even a vivid trouble in the emotional life and to recognise it so that they can harness that tempestuous thing to their drive—their fervour and love for God and man. Strong emotions make strong driving powers.

To take counsel with God and with others about the vital spiritual issues which have confronted them in their personal lives in their service abroad is the chance that the first furlough gives them. Their work blotted out so much of God. They had so little time, but now they have time, and that is why first furlough is such a strategic time. We are suffering terribly from a kind of Christian insipidity; suffering too from a Christianity which is merely conversion, merely service, when the goal set before us is perfection and we dare not let any life settle on a less true foundation than that 'high calling' of which St Paul was so aware.

The soldier in the thick of the battle has not time in which to consider his tactics or to clean his weapons—he just fights on and on as seems best at the moment. Afterwards, when it is over he can consult with his superior officer about his mistakes and ways of fighting better in the future. Therefore it is necessary when young missionaries come home, to have time for quiet thought and for seeking the guidance of someone further on in the spiritual adventure than they are themselves, who can, where it is necessary, help them to sort out the tangled strands of their past experience and give them real advice and guidance for the future.

If, on the other hand, at this really critical point in their development they are absorbed when on furlough in a succession of meetings where they have to give an account of their experiences abroad before they have had time to reflect upon those experiences, they can very easily do themselves real harm. With a gathering of people in front of them who are expecting to hear something really definite from them they are obliged to produce something, the usual result being that they talk at length about what seem the successful things, and thereby in the end they may cover up failures by partial success. After a few weeks of this their minds are already busied again with their work; they have been caught up into the home side of the missionary activity by persons at home, and the golden opportunity for a really detached period of 'looking back with God' has vanished. The rest of the furlough is swallowed up in the claims of friends, relatives, farewell meetings, etc., during which it is easy to forget all about failures. They may not even remember them until they are again back on their station facing the same difficulties, finding themselves no further on, perhaps failing in the same things again.

Another temptation, just as dangerous, though not as obvious, as meetings and deputation work, is the absorption of their energies on the more strictly academic and practical sides of training for their work. Almost every missionary needs a further training either in medical or educational work or in some special branch of these, and it is important that this should be fitted in during the furlough, but it must never be allowed to take the place of further spiritual training which is our most urgent need. The only hope is in the growing recognition of the primary importance of this period of spiritual readjust-ment and renewed vision in the lifework of the ambassador for Christ, and here some very clear thinking has to be done about what is real vocation. If they go out primarily to do medical work, then obviously the first claim on their time when they come home is the renewal of their medical knowledge and consultation with those doctors who can help them in their work on the field. If they go out *primarily* as ambassadors for Christ and primarily to show Him to the world, then surely the first claim to their time and energies is this period of readjust-ment to Him and fresh vision of Him, and nothing must be allowed to take its place. Whatever their means of expressing Him may be, whether as doctor, or nurse or teacher, the spiritual renewal *must* come first and the other courses second.

It had become increasingly clear to Florence what kind of people missionaries needed to be. She noted the essential qualities in a memorandum.

They must have a real hunger and thirst for God and a faith that works. The great present need in the work overseas was for people who have the capacity to *see*. Enough care was not being taken to conserve the potential prophets and seers. Too many were being wasted by the drive of organizations and institutions. The supreme need was to put *quality* into the work.

Missionaries must have the distinctive qualities of a Christian —humility and receptiveness. 'These are not virtues that one may either have or be without. They are the *conditions* of the Christian life.'

Missionaries must be disciplined enough to be getting on the top of their own personal difficulties and problems. 'If the Christian life is not a conquering life it is not present at all.' Since 'only two forces drive the world—love and hate', missionaries must be people with some fire of love who have achieved some positive success in living with other people in real Christian friendship.

The growth of these essential qualities could be greatly furthered, Florence believed, by the quiet facing of failures in the first term of missionary service in a further period of preparation during furlough. The possibility of providing something of this kind began to take definite shape while she was at Selly Oak. In February, 1940 she adumbrated what was in her mind in a circular letter to her old students.

I want to do something [she wrote] where I can still go on serving you with what I have of experience and real caring for you. I have a dream of a house in some lovely quiet place where you could come and be quiet and rest and read and talk —where things could be refreshed and recreated before you went off to your new courses and your other furlough adventures. And I should like it to be open for home people as well who needed to stop and know God again.

It is a dream, and there is no material hope of it happening, but perhaps it may because I think it would fulfil a need, and I feel it so very strongly. I visualise a central house and one or two warm cosy huts in the garden, far enough away from each other to be really alone, and where you could play the gramophone if you wanted without disturbing others. And there would be a Quiet Room for you to use as you liked, and nothing forced so that you could be pagan for a bit if you needed that! And lots of books, all kinds, and a place where you could do handwork. I believe that as the need for spiritual leadership becomes more and more urgent, as it is doing, we shall have to keep times of quiet and re-creation and being still to know God, not only on first furlough but on every furlough. Also for church people at home who go on and on and on in the same rut.

How this impossible dream took material shape is told by Florence herself in the chapters that follow.

Another thought, not explicitly mentioned in the letter that has just been quoted, was pressing itself increasingly on her attention, and its realization became the dominant aim of the St Julian's experiment. From the time of the crisis that had occurred in Uganda, Florence had been learning new lessons in the meaning of love. She now felt the need of moving forward to a further stage. Whereas the ordinary Christian lives the Christian life up to a certain point, there was need of a centre where some would make the attempt to break past the point at which most people stop. What that involved must be left to Florence to relate.

PART II

THE ST JULIAN'S COMMUNITY

by Florence Allshorn

VII

ORIGINS

TO THE QUESTIONS which are constantly asked about St Julian's it is never easy to give a short and simple answer. The roots go far back and what now is seems to have grown to a large extent of itself. Parts of it cannot rightly be understood apart from the whole.

Having been for some time a missionary in Africa, I was engaged for twelve years in training missionaries. I realized during that time that a second period of learning and thinking was necessary if the spiritual aim was to be kept alive and fruitful in the mission field in the face of all that threatened to oust it from the central place. I am sure that similar difficulties are met with by the young church worker or social worker at home, though more help may be available for them in facing their problems.

The situation for which a remedy was needed can perhaps best be explained by quoting a statement prepared by three young missionaries:

The general idea of the first tour seemed to be idealism or the doing of a job well, with little or no realisation that being in another country and labelled at long last 'missionary' was not in itself sufficient to make one a missionary. The farewell meetings, the goodbyes of friends and the garlanded welcome ahead all help to give importance and make self the centre of the picture. Disillusionment on arrival, pressure of overwork, lack of time, ignorance of language, climate, and tiredness, as well as difficult relationships with colleagues, produced confusion and the desire for escape. Some escaped outwardly into social life, into contacts with government officials, and other interests, whilst others escaped inwardly into a world of unreality. All knew they were failing, the difference being that some blamed their colleagues and the situation, others blamed themselves. Some grew hard, aggressive and reserved, others tamed and complacent, and yet others bewildered and lost. Whatever the tendency had been in England, it became exaggerated during the first tour abroad.

None of the three of us were ready for a second tour without more training. We were saved from a too easy self-satisfaction with what we had done in the job itself by some small spark of divine discontent, mercifully put into us in training.

This may be supplemented by a passage from an account of her experience by a young missionary chosen almost at random from among a number of statements of a similar kind:

I was an idealist, and wanted to rescue many souls from darkness to light. I knew that I wanted to marry, and would have preferred infinitely to have stayed in England, but having decided to go to India, I thought it was a single-minded decision for God. I wanted to evangelise in the sense of talking, and was expecting conversions. Probably I saw myself as the centre of light. During training, we had been told much about learning on the first tour, and about patience and understanding, but I thought of quick, immediate results and of easy victories for myself. I thought I knew how to work in a team, but I found I couldn't.

Climate, loneliness, isolation, languages, relationships were unbelievably hard, in fact nothing was easy, so that I was faced with a very sharply defined issue—God or failure. I chose God, but I did not know until years afterwards that what I thought was God was idealism and absolute standards; and that when I thought I was following Jesus, I was merely pleasing my own ideal of Him. I came from India still convinced that I was right and others wrong, and that failure in relationships was their fault, not mine. I do not think I was in the least humbled, only very strained indeed, with unrealised ideals and spoilt relationships, blaming the people who located me to the hospital to which I had been sent, but not seeing my own sin.

We were all of us in greater or less degree disturbed by the mediocrity of our witness to the rule of Jesus Christ, and we knew that the only way to surmount it was a more determined insistence on making faith, hope and love more real in our lives.

When we first begin to follow Christ's way of life, our knowledge of it is very embryonic and elementary, and yet we are inclined to think that we have the whole secret. We regard it as unnecessary to train ourselves in those sensitizing obediences which are the condition of receiving the heavenly grace that alone brings the flower and the fruit. Faith, hope and love have to be learned with infinite patience through a long time. They are the demands of a Creator who knew what He would have us be. We cannot pursue them feebly and attain in the Christian life. They are supreme ends which we cannot allow to be crowded out of our lives by a host of lesser purposes.

Faith, for example, as Jesus understood it, was a weapon with which to fight against principalities and powers, against the ruler of great darkness. Whatever names men have given to the power of darkness, its works are apparent to all. Faith, Jesus said, is a weapon which makes Satan fall from heaven. It is the triumphant cry of the conquering warrior and, when it is present, there is no room for hesitation or fear. Are we not tragically ignorant of its meaning? Do we not need to be trained in it? It is a shameful degradation of this great spiritual weapon, when we reduce its immensity to a means of overcoming some small difficulty which the ordinary man gets over without calling upon faith at all.

And so also with love. Deep in our bones we are conscious that we know almost nothing of the inexorable will to love that is an answer to a command. We have hardly begun to learn to distinguish it from our human ways of loving. How can we, when our hearts are so fretted by the stubborn self-centredness of our time? We know that what Nietzsche said is true:

And this hypocrisy found I worst among them, that even they that say they have the virtue of love, feign that virtue . . . it is mediocrity though it be called love, and ye shall perish of your many petty virtues. Too much yielding to yourselves, that is your soil. But for love to grow tall, like a tree, it must wind hard roots round hard rocks. Oh that ye would renounce half-willing.

Similarly Dostoevsky says with reference to the love of Jesus
Christ:

Such love is a possession dearly bought with much labour and
in a long time. You pay for it in blood and tears as you pay
for liberty. Jesus died because of love, but what do you and I
know about it? We who prattle of love, blind as to what it is,
reducing it to some small hum-drum notion of being kind. To
suppose that it is a quality which we can call up and use, when
and as we like between the rising up of the sun and its going
down, and then to talk from this common habit of mind about
the love of Jesus, or the love of God or any such love, is an
offence, almost a blasphemy.

That we are commanded to love, and cannot, is our dilemma
and our despair. But, as Kierkegaard said, 'even despair is a
choice'. It is a choice which we continually try to evade.

I and one other member of the present Community were
working in the early days of the war, at Selly Oak, to which the
training college for women missionaries of the Church Missionary
Society had been evacuated on its outbreak. Out of a multitude
of thoughts and much discussion one thought began to stand out
with growing clearness. Missionaries whom I had trained were
coming home, all longing, though some only vaguely, for a
place of quiet. There seemed nowhere to escape from the press of
life, the demands of families, the manifold temptations involved in
deputation work, nowhere quietly to face themselves, their
failures to live up to anything approaching the vision with which
they went out, nowhere to read and pray in peace. Though there
were many opportunities for meeting others of like mind, such as
conferences and study weeks, nowhere could they work out with
other people the really important things of the spiritual life, such
as tackling the roots of themselves and their relationships with
other people.

There was also at the back of our minds the tentative urge
towards community. This urge appeared to be touching many
different people in many different ways. In the past the emphasis
for those trying to live a more dedicated Christian life had been on
the need for an unusual effort to alter situations single-handed.

Now the leading of the Spirit seemed to be that the witness of living together a truly Christian life was more needed than solitary greatness. There was in it a much greater demand to die to oneself. There was in it much less personal prestige, and it seemed in those days to be an exciting adventure. It was too, we believed, the answer to the problem of difficult relationships which the world so greatly needed.

The two of us asked a third to join us, and we started to plan what we should do, and who should do what. We talked and made plans and dreamed dreams. All these plans and ideals were abandoned in the very early days, and it is difficult now to remember even what they were. The 'scheme' as we called it remained for many months an exciting idea. Somewhere underneath, however, we knew it was a great deal more serious than merely an excitement; we believed the thought was from God.

We got into touch with estate agents who sent us particulars of houses, and we spent our free days combing the Cotswold country for possible places to start. We had no money, no support from anyone at that time, but we had a strong urge to start the search. I resigned from being principal of the C.M.S. women's training. One of the two others had to choose between the 'scheme' and returning to India, and the other between this and a good post with the Young Women's Christian Association.

We started searching in the early days of 1940, and went on throughout that year. It was the year of the blitz on London, and for most of the year we went our several ways, but the search went on. In the first few days of 1941 two of us set out in a small car saying we would not return until we had found somewhere to start. Our searching brought us one freezing evening to Oakenrough in Haslemere. This was to be our first place of experiment. It was a house which had been left by an old lady's will for a purpose near enough to ours to make it possible for us to use it, as a beginning.

We found one other who said she would come for a year to cook, and the four of us moved in during Easter, 1941.

VIII

THE START

OAKENROUGH was a wooden house built on a very steep hillside
(so that the front entrance was upstairs) with five bedrooms,
five 'cells' outside, and half a cottage. We made the smallest room
into a library, and had a drawing-room, dining-room and sitting-
room. We had a most pleasant kitchen with an Aga stove, no
sanitation, and an attractive attic with a balcony, from which
you could see for thirty miles, and we made this into a chapel.
With a great sense of adventure we settled in. Then we opened our
doors most tentatively to our first guests. Our average number
was eleven or twelve, and a record was sixteen.

It was an inconvenient house to run, and there was a lot of need
to 'fit-in', but the surroundings were superb. It was built in a
wood, and surrounded by glorious walks. The kitchen faced south
and was full of sun, and the four of us lived there, played there,
cooked there, and did much of our battling there.

At this time most of our guests were war-tired people coming
for relaxation and rest. There were not many missionaries able
to get home, so the training side of the community did not develop
much at Oakenrough. We opened our doors to small conferences
which we always enjoyed having. Dr Oldham's Moot was one
of the first and most interesting. The Secretariat of the Church
Missionary Society came regularly for its meetings and has
continued to do so.

Those of us who embarked on the new venture were woefully
ignorant. Looking back in the light of what we even already see,
we were vividly green.

I think the great obstacle was, both in ourselves and others, that we were people of our generation and had few disciplines and obediences. We had vague and expansive feelings for some people and active dislikes for others. We had many words about fellowship but we had yet to put words into deeds, and we little knew what that would entail. The whole secret of the salvation of anything or anybody hinges on the conversion of words into deeds, with and through the whole being. There is in reality no absolute salvation, only infinite realms of experience providing more and more tests demanding more and more faith. It cannot be rammed home often enough that what is disastrous is the divorce between mind and action and that the ultimate can only be experienced in action.

It is side-stepping of that fact that is the explanation of the silent disasters among the Christians of the present day and their failure to live in community together. It was so in our case. We defended ourselves and we justified ourselves. But there came a time when we had to face ourselves for the disorderly mass of individuals that we were. I believe we all have to face that before we can begin even to start the race towards something better.

That brought us to another point. We were in no sense aware of the special kind of courage such a course would exact from us. We had not been bred to anything in the nature of heroism in our Christian upbringing. Indeed the heroism of Christianity has been lost sight of in something we have made comfortable, because compromising. But such a flattened state of spiritual compromise will 'stab no spirit broad awake'. We need some kind of a large and costly vision before we can rouse our determination to live in accordance with it. However small our vision is at the beginning, the necessity lies upon us to be faithful to it, and to accept no defeat in reaching after it.

We have all to discover that the wisdom of Jesus Christ is not an isolated religious wisdom; that it is the wisdom of One who knew why and of what we are made. The wisdom by which the life of Jesus Christ was ruled and which made Him the first-born among many brethren is at the same time the law of the universe. We had to learn that by no other path could we attain to the fulfilment of created being. The analogy of the seed dying to produce the tree is inescapably true, and 'dying to self' is the only

F

way in which the new person can come to birth. And dying to self exacts an infinite courage.

Perhaps some of us have to learn it the hard way. I had so to learn it myself in my experience as a missionary in Uganda.[1] I have seen one woman, who knew she had denied Christ, weep the night through, and it is such experiences that teach a young thing more than all the sermons in the churches. That I happened to be that person is neither here nor there, but I did see how, if one person could forget herself and call on God in any situation, that was the condition through which He could come. It was the things I saw in those very gruelling years that gave me the vision of what we needed to learn in our Community. It was the fact that I *knew* these things by bitter experience that gave me some ground for leading such an experiment as this has been.

Those who embarked on the new experiment were not chosen because of any special qualifications for carrying out a venture of this kind. I did not know at the start what it was we were going to try to work out. I knew that, if our primary need was to learn how to obey the first commandment, there was equal need to learn to practise the second. We might be tempted to think that we were obeying the first because of the work we were doing, but we ought not to be in any doubt whether we were obeying the second. It was in obedience to the second that every one, Christian and non-Christian alike, was failing. No one seemed to know a way of getting beyond the check that comes in personal relationships and makes them such an eternal defeat. The best that could be achieved seemed to be to become resigned to the others' difficulties of temperament. Whether it was marriage or any other relationship, the result appeared to be the same.

Perhaps the overseas communities of two or three people working on a mission station brought things to a head and made them more obvious than at home, because there were not other people to pick and choose from, and there was no means of avoiding those you did not get on with. Though we knew that we had always been defeated by personal relationships, and had all had experience of that defeat at home and abroad, we set out

[1] Pp. 27–9.

blithely to solve the problem. We were, as I have said, very green and did not realize the deep selflessness that was required from everyone. We were overloaded with self-centredness to an extent that we only began to realize when we got going. What kept us together was not the fact that we immediately got on with one another. We did not. What carried us through was that we had said that we would not leave if we found ourselves in a bad patch, and that we would not accept defeat.

We were not people possessing special capacities. We had, so far as I can see, distributed between us a fairly high standard of order and beauty, something of the spirit of sacrifice, a lot of good will in the determination to make the experiment, some real bits of humility, a capacity for vision and a fair share of vitality and tenacity. On the other hand, there was self-centredness, slip-shoddiness in spirit, mind and behaviour, pride and the emotional dishonesty which is part of the make-up of most human beings. We learned to recognize instability in ourselves, and to hate it. But even when we hate, there is in us a terrible self-defensiveness which clings on to what we loathe. Not even yet have we come clearly to the point of saying 'My fault, my own fault, my own most grievous fault', but we are nearer to it and sometimes we reach it. That is the place where things begin to become straight between us. That kind of honesty seems to me the only thing to prize.

One of us is rather slip-shod and casual, and another is very orderly and meticulous. Can you imagine what they have to get through when it is a matter of setting and serving trays together? For a long time they lived in a state of exasperation and we always knew when they were on the job together. The kitchen was full of a kind of pent anger. But it isn't there any longer; they have found their way through that bit of the clash of warring elements.

It is only as you know yourself moving forward a little or climbing upward, that you dare face yourself as you are, and you can open out what you *were* without fear. I think we would say that what we thought we were was a very different picture from what we found ourselves to be. We had a really ghastly amount of self-centredness among us, pride enough to stiffen everything that was gentle and good for years, as well as lesser soul-sicknesses. The scene as it presented itself to me was not so much that of a group of people possessing un-Christlike qualities, as of an arena in which devilish things in us fought against the things in us that were good and sane and sweet. These contrary forces inhabited all of us in some degree, and when the fight was on we stumbled and fell. We went through some dreadful destructive moments. We sometimes longed to chuck it and run. But we didn't, and we found ourselves learning things as we went along.

It needs something of an effort to recall those early days. We planned out our parts. A—— was to cook, B—— was to run the house, C—— to help there and in the garden, D—— well, D—— was me, and my part was to lead everything spiritual, mental and practical, till everyone 'took on'.

A—— came to pieces as cook because we found she had no sense of smell and very little of taste, and we suffered being over-peppered or under-salted patiently, but not for long. There was a re-shuffle, and C——, on the prestige of having had once a term's course in high-class cookery, went into action with everything to cook with except anything that could be called in any way high-class. However she did manfully, only she was a muddler, and the kitchen looked like the scene of some disaster when the bell rang for dinner each day. A——, who was very kind-hearted, flung herself into the mêlée and restored order each day at 12.30, but C—— went on cheerfully piling up dirty sauce-pans and every kind of utensil, taking it for granted it could go on for ever. But A——'s work was increasing and was beginning to be a whole-time job in itself, and C——, taking her help for granted, began to make her feel fed-up.

Then the crisis came. A—— overheard C—— talking very piously to a younger person about love being thoughtfulness for the other, and to crown the outrageous irrelevance, C—— took prayers that night and pressed home the same virtue. It was too much. A—— stumped out of prayers, and words flew.

Those were the kind of differences that split us in those early days, and no one puts those kind of habits to rights all at once. We were always making each other angry because we were not responsible enough in our own jobs, which after all were very new to us, and not thoughtful enough about other jobs. Those who suffered from these tensions were people who had previously got on quite well with others in ordinary relationships. It was only when we refused to lower our standards and to be content with easy adjustments at the surface level that we found how addled a mass of unsanctification we were in our feelings. How could we ever describe it? We were all theoretically aware of what we ought to be because we were perforce a training community. Others were coming in with their problems of living, which were just the same as ours, and we did not want to talk theory with them. We wanted to talk from knowledge and to be real, because we had fought past the particular thing in our own make-up that was holding them back from happiness and harmony in life. But differences of temperament went very deep and were as stubbornly rooted as the habits of years could make them. In fairness to ourselves, we had set ourselves some job. It is more difficult than one imagines to fuse together four women, all of whom have had jobs of their own and been supreme in them, in the common running of one show. In a note I made at the time I wrote this:

It all becomes so vivid—the insistence of Jesus Christ that He was the Way and His prayer that 'they all may be one'. I truly believe that we shall become a 'rejoicing company' as He hoped and prayed His followers would. When we are for a few moments really with Him we have a special kind of quietness, and when we are pulling together over something the whole thing becomes creative in a new way. But there is this horrid habitual drag of ourselves, and our languid love for Him, and this stupid helplessness before our own feelings and I am sometimes overwhelmed with dismay. Really in the light of what we say we know, we seem to be the very embodiment of insincerity and discomfort; but perhaps I am too impatient.

When people talk about starting communities we look at each other. They seem to us like people starting for the North Pole without even knowing that they need a warm coat. At the risk of repetition I will let one of the others speak of those first two years.

Perhaps we were no more and no less than the ordinary person. Perhaps others will recognise that a 'sterile fact' like the following can happen. We write it down after a long deliberation. It is not something easy to write down even though it seems now far away. We write it down because we want to tell people that they can get beyond these frustration points; that no one could be worse than we were; that we can give them a hope because we are finding our sure way through; that no one need be frustrated and beaten at any like point; and that for the Christian witness of this day we must not allow ourselves to be beaten. It is this kind of impossible and miserable contact that destroys so much of what could be good building for God. People either leave the group or job, or carry on with the unhappy tangle going on underground.

We had talked quite a lot in study-groups and retreats about what, as far as we could see, 'to love others as He had loved us,' meant. We could talk quite thoughtfully and we *felt* sincerely, but next morning such a scene as this could happen:

A——: (aggressive, very tidy, dominating, insensitive to her effect on others, nervously unbalanced, a bad sleeper, coming into the kitchen): 'The larder (B——'s job) is disgusting.'

B——: (impractical, untidy, supersensitive to criticism, quickly on the defensive): 'You never notice anything that is clean. I spent quite a long time cleaning the bottles: all you notice is the larder which was done yesterday, but I haven't had time to do it to-day.'

A——: 'It's no use arguing: the larder is disgraceful. It is against the thing we are trying to work out.'

B——: 'Well I went upstairs yesterday and your linen room was disgracefully untidy. You're so fundamentally unjust.'

A——: 'You will never learn, nor take anything, always throw the blame back on the other person.'

B——: 'How could anyone learn from anyone who is so self-righteous? You're like a mistress talking to a maid.'

A——: 'It is no use, you will not learn.'

So it would go on. The occasions were small, but they increased the tension that had grown up between them. They tried to clear it up, but it took months for them to get away from the usual escape of the trouble being the other's fault, and each to see her own part in it with greater detachment and

more clearly. These and other crises like them were the
beginning. We got baffled, perplexed, and in despair.

The fact that nothing could be hidden in such close contact,
that everything came into the light, made the struggle extremely acute. When the contact from which it seems impossible to unclamp came to a certain stage, we met and talked
it over, and started again. We prayed, but we could get no
answer to prayer until we saw our own fault disentangled
from the sin of the other which *seemed* to have caused our outraged feelings, and as I say, we escaped that for months.

Slowly we learnt together to bring the frustrated contacts
to the light so that others could show us the real truth of them,
and the faults on each side, and as we honestly then tried to deal
with them we won something which is rooted and grounded,
something from which we can only grow straight.

I have said that from the beginning we set before us as our
fundamental aim to learn the meaning of the two great commandments. What this meant in practice I will leave another of
the members of the original community to explain in her own
words:

Everyone, we suppose, builds up his or her life with some
picture of himself. Some people are quite a lot like the picture
they build, some are a little like it, and some not at all. But no
one *knows* himself until the picture is challenged and perhaps
broken altogether. It really was a terrible time, this breaking up
of the pictures we had each made for ourselves. At times it
seemed intolerable. We knew hate, and malice, and that dreadful desire to hit back hard if we had been hurt. We found things
buried in ourselves which were really shocking. Such deep
resentment perhaps that one knew one could not forgive, and
yet saying every day the Lord's Prayer. There was the misery
caused by pride that refused to give in, and yet we chose that
misery rather than give in. There was jealousy of a pretty
virulent kind, and cynicism, when it appeared that another
was being praised when you felt that *you* knew what she was
really like. We were new to this, and we had no pattern.
It was the carving out of the pattern that was the grimmest part.
One either had to give up in bitterness or resentment, or one
had to find a way through. We had come to a place where it

was impossible in our own strength to forgive. But we have never said 'Peace, peace, where there is no peace', and we have risked conflict all the time in order to find peace of a true kind *at the other side of conflict*. The devil, or devils, fight hardest when they are being attacked, so we discovered. Since those first shattering years we are finding a way, we are finding that there is something, more resembling love as it is usually conceived. We know there is no peace, whatever kind of a façade they put on, for people who somewhere inside themselves have a fear of being known. They must break through this fear, no matter at what cost, if they are going to have any message for this generation.

In the ways that have been described we come to understand that the Word which became flesh does not express itself so much in teaching, lecturing or pastoral work as in the moment lived in Him, whatever you may be doing. The kitchen (because we mostly gathered there) and the house were for us the arenas where we fought and fell or fought and conquered; we witnessed there unconsciously and only when self was not there. Some of us were good at taking prayers, others at talking in study groups, others at practical work, but it was in none of these things as such, it was in the actual attitude and deed over a saucepan, or in your quality of thinking of someone else, whether you took sides or healed the separation between sides that was the actual test. You can sit in your principal's room, or before your class, and talk with real earnestness, but the great things are not won like that. Humility, generosity, peace-making only rise from the actually controlled deed, the love-restrained re-action, the detached from self sight of truth in a situation in which the truth is not pleasant for you. In the actual working together you have to change your natural self-guarding laziness and carelessness if you are to live at peace. The adventures are endless and it is a continual actual choosing whether you go the way of self or the way of love. You cannot cover over what you are by any amount of brilliant talk, even spiritual talk. We could talk in the chaple without the guilt of hypocrisy only as we lived in the house.

IX

THE COMMUNITY

IT HAS already been made clear that the impelling motive in making the new venture was a sense of the need of learning in deep experience the meaning of community. Is the movement towards community, the desire for closer fellowship in small groups, which is so widely felt to-day, an essential part of the Christian way of life, or is it merely something subsidiary? In the more recent past Christian people have tended to think of fellowship as a delightful consequence of Christian living rather than as an integral part of it. As a result fellowship has too often ceased to be either Christian or delightful. It has become stale and stereotyped. We are aware that the root of fellowship is Christ's second commandment, but we refuse to go deep enough.

In our day obedience to the second commandment has found, perhaps, its chief expression in humanitarian movements—in the desire to serve rather than to love and understand. We have become excellent social servants, Christian organizers, doctors, nurses, teachers, but we have lost the essential spring of 'fellowship one with another'. People outside Christianity look at our little Christian groups, our parish churches, our Christian schools, colleges, societies, and fail to see them shining out like light in dark places. Christian committees, diocesan councils, missionary bodies, all these should be centres of light, of the Spirit—and so often they are not. Instead of 'How these Christians love one another' we hear 'I never go near church societies or parish organizations, there is so much gossip and rivalry'. The criticism would not matter if it were not so often the truth.

Jesus said, 'Where two or three are gathered together in my name, there am I in the midst.' Why have we failed so often to realize that promise? Why do we see men and women who start so well fall back between thirty and sixty, clinging on to power and position for its own sake, not for God's, becoming afraid of what others will think, afraid to think honestly or to live fully? Why does this process happen so often to Christians who should be our real leaders, and happen particularly in our present age? Why is the Church not producing saints in anything like the numbers that advancing knowledge and our inexhaustible spiritual resources might lead us to expect?

One reason, no doubt, is that the subtle temptations of modern life keep us from obedience to the first commandment. The emphasis upon worldly success and individual independence has side-tracked us from the really single-minded love of God. We have let our values get muddled. We have allowed the rush and busyness of life to stifle our contact with God. We have not time enough for the higher adventure.

A second reason is that modern life has, on the whole, taken us away from community—from all really close contact with our fellow-Christians. The parish group, the school group, the family group, all still exist, but there is an ever lessening obligation to them. We can escape them so easily, if we want to. Even when we work together as Christians in a big enterprise, a diocesan council or a missionary society, we do not live together, nor do we meet for our leisure time. We can escape. Thus we have little or no machinery for learning to 'love our neighbour as ourselves' in the deeper sense. We are never, or rarely, forced to come to grips with ourselves or with each other in any vital relationship, because there is no one (except perhaps our own family) to whom we have sufficient sense of obligation.

I have already described through what bitter experiences and at what cost those of us who started the Community had to learn the lesson for ourselves. But we knew that our need was shared by many others. In particular, we had in mind the need of returning missionaries for a place of quiet where they could re-equip themselves for their work.

To return to the college where they had first been trained would not meet their real needs. To go back to student life would not be good for the missionary herself. Her need was to become more adult. The reason why she needed further training was that she had come short in the task to which she had been called, and she could not address herself single-mindedly to what she was not if students around her kept looking up to her and lauding her for what she was. We needed a centre for more mature people, where they would also meet with those engaged in other types of work, e.g. church and social workers at home, and, it might be, visitors from other countries.

That we were right in our estimate of the need is shown by the fact that women of all ages, from the younger missionary on her first furlough to the older woman of fifty, have come to us and that we have had twice to move to a larger house. We are always full and are usually booked for weeks ahead.

Those who come to us come increasingly for longer periods and one society at least has come to attach so much importance to this further training as to grant longer furloughs for this purpose. This was at first looked on as impossible in view of the urgency of the needs abroad. But this view has given place to the more far-sighted wisdom that a year wisely spent in further training makes all the difference to the life and work of a missionary in the years to come. The young man or young woman of to-day has nothing like the stability of character of the older missionary, and account must be taken of this. The young to-day live in a different and more bewildering world and they need time to find their steady feet. A short preliminary training cannot enable them to do that, except in the case of a very few. The need for further training is felt also by many of the younger men, but the number of those who are given the opportunity is much smaller as yet than in the case of women.

We have often been asked why those who have been converted and had a spiritual experience need more training. There are exceptional people who have an early spiritual development and are able to find their way through difficulties through some inner capacity which most of us lack. But experience shows that these are the merest handful in comparison with the many hundreds who cannot without help find a steadfast centre for their lives.

Does this mean that in the past Christian training has been inadequate? Undoubtedly. There has been in recent times a growing concern for the education of the body, of the mind, of the emotions. But nothing like the same eagerness has been manifested for the education of the spirit. The whole set-up of the Church has missed spiritual education. Yet spiritual education is co-extensive with life itself; it is the education of the living spirit within us. This part of us is left to pick up what education it can. But the mediocre Christianity which we see around us shows quite plainly that few people can pick up their spiritual education in this haphazard manner. Our spirit is in fact being educated by all that presses in on us, but, if left to chance, it may be a bad education. Those who take the Christian witness seriously cannot but be concerned about the immature Christianity of to-day. Most people after receiving some stimulation of thought and emotion from sermons and being given some preparation for confirmation are led to believe that, if they take their Communions regularly, all will be well. They are given little guidance about integrating their outward obediences into an inner integrity. Because of the lack of education in the realm of real experience they do not learn to overcome arrests in spiritual growth nor to avoid lapses into spiritual inertness.

There has perhaps never been a time when to the same extent the absorption of undigested matter has been combined with fine but abstract and empty thinking. We have surrendered to intellectualism, and spiritual growth has been taken for granted. The right use of discipline, social patterns of conduct, the redirection of habits, and ways of co-operative living together are not given the same attention nor are they as carefully and scientifically directed as intellectual instruction. The reason is not far to seek. Various reasons have led to a policy of expansion at the cost of thoroughness, and encouraged a type of education which is concerned with imparting a knowledge of various 'subjects', rather than the intensive mastery of a few basic Christian obediences and principles. The emphasis in the present curriculum is too often on the acquisition of a knowledge of formulated truth rather than on developing the student's capacity to discover spiritual truth. Any college which does not put examination results first will not be regarded as successful in the eyes of the world, and the Church itself is too apt to judge things also by the standards of worldly success.

Why is it that the Church has given so little help in spiritual education? It has a wonderful heritage of Christian doctrine, and there is much devoted exposition of it. The reason surely is that doctrine must always be related to experience, and that the test of apprehension of a doctrine is willingness to put it to the proof in our own lives. Within the period of a single day we may penetrate more deeply into the meaning of the incarnation, the life, death and resurrection of Jesus, on condition that we make the first move to repentance and humility which is the gateway of entrance into the Kingdom. The complete movement is *repentance*, putting us into the right relationship of a state of humility and obedience before God; *incarnation*, the receiving of Jesus Christ and His forgiveness; *life* in following the way of Jesus, leading to the *death* of self; *resurrection* and the reception of the *Holy Spirit*. Any one who has known the release which comes from the death of self and the inflow of spiritual power which follows, knows that this is a real experience. This whole movement can take place within an hour. What follows is always a little more light, so that God and not self is glorified in heart and mind.

It might seem hardly necessary to say all this, but in point of fact people come to us who have never been taught the meaning of this relating and integrating. Neither multitudes of sermons nor faithful attendance at Communion necessarily *integrate* truth. When we awaken to what an undiluted Christianity means, we recognize ourselves to be the blindest creatures on earth.

The root from which the weaknesses in modern Christianity spring is pride. As Christians, and followers of Jesus Christ, we have not taken pride half seriously enough. But the Devil has. The Devil knows that as long as he can control human pride, it does not matter how many prayer meetings, how many services, how much devotion goes on; he can still wreck any group of Christians sooner or later and frustrate God's purposes for them and for the world. For the Devil's purpose a proud Christian is of much more use than an atheist or a pagan.

There are many kinds of pride—personal ambition, love of power, or just the independence of spirit which refuses to be touched, self-sufficiency, pride in our Christian character. Pride militates against the one intrinsic necessity for the mature achievement of 'Not I but Christ'. We have even divested the word humility of its true meaning and we will not see that to build a superstructure of Christianity on any other foundation save humility is to build on sand.

What then is the remedy?

First, to return to the real single-minded desire to love God —chiefly in our day by getting time apart, giving time to God, giving Him a chance to speak to us.

Secondly, to join together in community, wherever we are, not necessarily creating new groups, but rebuilding the old ones in college, parish, society; tightening up our relationships, demanding a high standard, giving up time to be together and to get to know each other, recognizing and acknowledging a relationship, a mutual need of each other in Jesus Christ.

Thirdly, there must be certain groups which are pioneers of community living and can show the way to the higher standard. These should normally have the stability which only a central house can give, as well as contact with the world in all its departments. The strength of the best medieval communities lay in their stability and their wide contacts. The 'specialized community' must have a condition of entry. There need not be poverty in possessions, but there *must* be poverty of spirit, the readiness to give, to share, to sacrifice personal pride and personal ambition, to lay down our gifts, our achievements, at each other's feet, just as the disciples laid their possessions.

Those who realize that in the Community we are finding our way into a new realm of life often want to know in what ways what we learn is transmitted to wider circles outside. We have had coming to us from time to time at least three hundred younger people in any given year. Most of them have done some work in the house with us, joined in study circles, and talked. Some of them formed themselves into groups who come four times a year for long week-ends and one full week. There are about eighty members of such groups, of whom more than half are missionaries who are going into all parts of the world and will all touch some small area where they work. The others go back into schools, colleges, hospitals and offices. They all take the same Bible study notes which are drawn up by us and are based on the two commandments, running through the different books of the

Bible, with a leading challenge to integrate it into actual daily life. These take for each week one small or larger paragraph from the Bible and keep the students at it for a week instead of the usual day. They do not of course take the place of reading of the Bible.

These wider circles are finding the same sure direction as ourselves, and each time they come back they have consolidated some new ground or become more uneasy over the old. It is all *moving*. Once touch the beginning of the rope of real Christian love and there is no possibility of becoming static. Morality can leave you stuck, but not love. It is only the lover who can say 'the greatest of all sinners am I', as St Paul did, not at the beginning of the adventure, but at the end. It is an endless sanctification because it breeds a real hunger and thirst after it. It never reaches its goal, it can only press on. Its growth is often very little conscious to the person concerned. It is dynamic. Every little act of humility and self-forgetfulness sheds light on the next step ahead and beckons forward. That is experienced fact; we know it, even though we have only the frayed ends in our hands as yet.

We sometimes meet the criticism that we have taken ourselves out of the world. No one who is serving a family has taken herself ✳ out of the world. Our family comes and goes like most grown-up families, but its needs have to be met. Anyone who has worked with us for a few months could bear this out. There are twenty-five people to be fed and cared for, twenty-five bedrooms to keep clean and tidy as well as the fair-sized house which goes with them. There are people to see, talk to and guide in their reading and study. There is shopping, washing, letters, mending, and all the hundreds of little interruptions which cannot be taped. It is difficult to fit in an extra meeting for the Community itself, should it be needed.

We begin at 7 a.m., and we get off to our rooms about 9 p.m. We have one free day a week each, and we are supposed to have from 2.30-4.0 p.m. free daily, but that is the time when our personal things have to be done. We are quite as busy as most people are, and it is a very exacting sort of busyness. We have either to nail down on a purpose or to be swept along by the 'job' on a line of least resistance. The Devil is just as busy here as he is anywhere in the world at large, and infinitely subtle in his ways of keeping us just not effective against him. I have worked in

a good many places, in slums, the mission field, colleges and offices
and I have never found him more active in my own life than he is
here. We are inclined to think of the 'world' as consisting of
buses and trams, offices and schools and hospitals, but the 'worldly
mind', which is the enemy of the spiritual, is everywhere and
incredibly difficult to escape from, here as well as everywhere else.

When the whole day is taken up with little distracting things
and little relationships, and when one person whom you are
feeling 'jagged' with looms gigantic on the horizon of the day,
it is difficult to keep any vision of the purpose of what we are
doing. It is often just at those times that unthinking people tell us
that we are in danger of being too enclosed, and that we are too
ignorant of what the world is like. The life of the house, the farm
and the children's house and the fields between, provide a rich
existence, and the lives of those who come to stay here enter into
ours and are all the time widening and enriching our experience.

The Community began and has continued as a community of
women. We started during the war. What was at the back of our
minds was the longing to find the way to peace. We happened
to be a group of women. We hoped that some man might join
and look after the training of men. Members of the Community receive no salaries, but only their board and a little pocket
money, and it is more difficult for men to work without salaries.
A younger man, who may want to marry, has to earn a salary.
As the number of women members grew, it became more difficult
for a single man to join. One young man has now dared to break
the vicious circle and has become engaged to one of the members,
and we shall have to face the question of their support.

It is possible that in the adventure of personal relationships
women are the best pioneers. Margaret Mead, the anthropologist,
has shown that women have certain advantages in the understanding of themselves and their fellow men and women, which comes
from generations of experience in home and family. But one
cannot generalize. One or two of the men who come to us have
just as eager a longing to know more as the women have. For
the most part, however, those trained in theological colleges are
inclined to be too dogmatic and to talk theory. They think we are
very far behind because of our attitude of 'We don't know it

all'. A good many men, of course, come for periods to share the life of the house and of the farm.

People quickly recognize that we have standards of good work, and we are sometimes asked what these have to do with the spiritual life. Everyone, it is suggested, is not necessarily good at practical work. But all can learn to work to a standard, and the peace and beauty of the house demands this. As Gutkind says, 'Not until perfection has been achieved in the lower spheres of life can there be peace in the higher'. Our life is all one whole. We cannot be slip-shod in any one part of us without its affecting the rest. The quality of work we do is the outcome of the mind. The carpentering Jesus did could not have been slip-shod or half-done.

There is always something which makes for peace in coming into a room that is orderly, with bright polished furniture, and always something that makes for distraction of mind in a room which is disorderly and with furniture smeared and dull. It is easy to sentimentalize about beauty, but we do not love it till we create it where we are. Some of us keep it in a department. We love it in nature, and in art perhaps, but we keep it there. But there is a scope for art and a chance to create whatever we do and wherever we are. Some of us have found it hard to see the importance of a well-kept house, but no one who has learnt to get past her normal casualness in 'loving beauty' has ever doubted that it was good to go through the distress of learning.

When people say to us, 'to be practical is not my job', we put them to *do* a practical job. By experience of the house, by study groups and example, they soon come to see that not to have a sense of pride and worthwhileness in the achievement is second-rate thinking. Everybody attains a standard in time. Some are slower than others. The teacher who has done nothing except teaching for years, or the casual, untidy person who thinks that anything will do as long as it is done, soon finds another part of her coming to life—a greater awareness of the beauty of order, and a delight in doing things with her hands. There is too the satisfaction of group-work, and of making the whole a completed thing for the sake of the people who are resting here from the disorder of the home where there is always too much to do and only one woman to do it.

G

X

EXPANSION

WE HAD not been long at Oakenrough before we found that we were having to refuse, on account of lack of space, too many people who urgently needed what we could give them, and our minds turned towards enlargement or moving.

At this time there was no thought of children, very little thought of enlarging the Community, and the first and only signs of a farm were the rabbits and goats.

Almost immediately we had the first thought that we must grow, things started to happen. One of us taking up *The Times* rather casually one day saw an interesting house on the front page. Upon enquiry we were told that it was £15,000, and having not more than a few hundred between us, we went off to Barns Green the next day to see the house. From the first it seemed to be the answer to our wonderings. Most fortunately the Bishop of Worcester was staying with us at the time, and he and other friends who had some idea of finance helped us to arrange a mortgage. Many would-be helpers advised us not to take on such a large responsibility at such a time (1943) but a few men and women of faith encouraged us to go ahead.

The whole venture seemed almost too big, but the right thing seemed to be to do all we could and see if we came to a final stop. We never did. Each alarming fence that loomed ahead was astonishingly surmounted. We had no furniture, except our own bits and pieces, no cutlery, no linen, as all we had had at Oakenrough was lent and of course had to be left behind with the house. And we had practically no money to buy any of these things.

We saw the advertisement in May, 1943, and to our astonishment found ourselves installed at the end of August. It was at this time that the Bishop of Worcester, who has been a friend and adviser all the time, suggested that it would be good to have a few friends to act as Trustees. A small body of Trustees was appointed with the Bishop as chairman. We found ourselves possessors of St Julian's, Barns Green, which we bought on a mortgage, for the sum of £12,500.

All through the miraculous happened. Several people who had their furniture in store lent us all they had. We had gifts of cutlery, china, and linen. We went to auction sales, and became acquainted with almost all second-hand dealers in the neighbourhood. Friends were more than generous in the help and gifts both in money and kind that they gave, and before very long we felt we could call our next annual review 'Experiment Established'. For so it was.

By this time the 'scheme' had grown into the Community. The name of the house we had bought was 'Batchelors', and it was clear to the least intelligent that this would hardly be suitable, so after much thought and discussion we called it St Julian's (after an ancient Sussex saint noted for hospitality) and so it has remained, and so it has become known.

Always good things came to us. It was necessary, having such a large place, to have a man for the garden, and for the odd jobs in the house and for the electric engine. We tried every possible avenue and had even approached the land army. But at that period of the war every able-bodied man was either in the forces or in essential industry. Not quite everyone, however, since one day, just before we all moved in, a man and his son aged ten arrived at the back door and announced that he was a gardener, and did we want one. We did. He is still with us and has become, with his son who now also works with us, an integral part of the house. Not only was he a gardener, but there was hardly any odd job that he could not do, and finally he set to and built a bungalow for himself and his family, starting with an old chicken house that we bought for him, at his request, for £20.

At first St Julian's seemed spacious beyond telling in comparison with Oakenrough, but we soon found ourselves expanding.

During 1944 and 1945 we had quite a lot of requests from tired parents to be allowed to come and bring their children. We always of course said 'No', as no house could remain quiet with children. We refused them very sorrowfully. We realized that parents, especially during those years of strain when help was almost unavailable, needed a quiet rest more than most. One day we were having tea in the Chapel garden (which we tried to keep as a private Community garden) with a group of friends, and we said not too seriously, 'Of course what we need now is a children's house.' Not too seriously, because there seemed no possible hope of achieving a children's house! Within about a month, however, of that tea, when we were on holiday, we heard to our astonishment that the farmer living at the next farm was putting his farm up for sale. There was a great demand for property then (1946), so we flew home from our holiday and looked at it and saw that it was the perfect place for children. It had a large playroom, and a bedroom the same size, that would hold at least eight small beds. The other rooms and two acres of garden were ideal.

But then, how could we buy it? How could we furnish it? Who would run it? How should it be financed?

Having experienced the really wonderful way that these sort of questions which seemed insurmountable had a habit of getting answered, we went ahead to see what would happen. We found someone who had just had a legacy left to her, who was able to buy the house and furnish it rather scantily. Again visits to second-hand shops and auction sales. Again people lending and giving odd necessary bits of furniture, and after a short time we found that we had enough to start. We started with a family of missionaries home on furlough who had children of their own. They lived there and took other children. It was all a great experiment, and we have had a lot to learn about what is good and what is not good for a children's house. This family returned to Africa and another came. This time the wife ran it while the husband trained for ordination. Many valiant people came and helped for varying lengths of time, and it has always been very hard work. It is quite a different problem from St Julian's. Not only is there all the housework and entertainment and supervision, but all one's energies are demanded at meal times, and an astonishing amount of washing, ironing and mending has to be done, that is not required for the guests at St Julian's. We have had children from two weeks old to sixteen years.

We started White Turret (as it was called) in 1946, and by the time we moved to Coolham it had more than found its place. We realize now that it is an inevitable and integral part of the Community. It has been full during all school holidays, and we have to turn many away in the summer. It was pleasantly full during the rest of the year, and this gives those who run it a slight 'let-up'. It would be impossible to go on during the whole year at the same pressure as the holiday times. We discovered that order was one of the most essential requisites for such a house, and one by one the right people have come and it has been a happy and lovely acquisition to the whole.

As the war ended, more and more missionaries came home, most of them in need of rest. Bit by bit they found that after they had rested they needed to have some way and place to put into practice the things they had learned, and so they came and worked and studied with us. Some came for a year, some for several months, some for weeks. This side of the work grew until there was almost no time when there were not several of these people, who for the want of a better name we called 'workers'. They began to work together as a group and they began to find it the most valuable part of their furlough. It was primarily for these people that we saw that a move to a larger place was essential. They had no sitting-room for themselves where they could meet and talk, and we were constantly having to ask them to move to allow for the many who had to be fitted in but for whom we had no room.

During the years at Barns Green the Community increased from four to twelve. We started after a while accepting people on probation for a year or more before they came right into the Community, and towards the end of our time there, we had services of admission both for the probationers and for those of them who became members of the Community.

We were able at Barns Green to provide for slightly larger conferences, and during our time there we were visited by people from America, Africa, China, Holland, Geneva, India,

France and Greece, and were kept in this way in touch with international Christian life and thought.

In October, 1949, after a fresh urge to move on, but before we had at all decided to look for new quarters, we were out one evening in the car searching for one of our dogs who had not been home for more than twenty-four hours. We passed a board announcing that a property, which was quite hidden from view, was for sale, and that it had four hundred and sixty acres, a lake, two farm-houses and thirteen cottages. Two of us the next day came to see it, and it became clear almost at once that this was quite probably to be our next home.

The house was bigger than Barns Green. It had three stories instead of two. It had a wonderfully open view to Chanctonbury Ring on the South Downs. The view from the house embraced terrace and lawns, a five acre lake with swans and ducks, open fields, and then perhaps ten miles of country to the South Downs. When we first saw it there seemed to be endless loose boxes, some of which were interlined, and all electrified. Loose boxes are always full of suggestions and possibilities! (As we write four of them have already been converted into a temporary Chapel.) There was a beautiful garden and the excellent kitchen garden looked fully able to feed the sixty of us (including the farm and children) who will need to be fed. There were avenues of herbaceous borders, many fruit trees, and seemingly every kind of shrub.

In comparison, the buying of St Julian's, Barns Green was child's play to the mountainous obstacles that faced us in the buying of St Julian's, Coolham. The first day that we saw it the figure of £50,000 was mentioned. This was a staggering amount. Although we were all pretty buoyant about it from the beginning, the first bridge to be crossed was to persuade the Trustees that it was even a remote possibility. Having wired our Chairman that there was a crisis (most unfortunately the telegram arrived in the middle of the night by 'phone) three of the Community followed up the telegram by a visit to Worcester. The Bishop, being a man of faith, hope and experience, agreed at least to call a Trustees' meeting, and so they came to see us and the proposed house and to discuss possibilities. After much careful thought, and an anxious night, we all found ourselves the next day in agreement that we should offer £50,000, and under no circumstances more.

The next day a visit was paid to the owner of the house and the offer made in person. The owner even at that time had had a higher offer, but she appeared to like the purpose we had for the house more than the purpose of her other hopeful purchaser. We rejoiced that night as though the house was really ours. Little did we know!

Then we started on a prolonged neck and neck race against seemingly impossible odds, for just as we were starting to consider what to do next, we were unofficially informed that even though our offer had been accepted, unless we had paid the deposit by a certain date the whole property would be auctioned. We could not pay the deposit of £5,000 until we could be sure that we could settle on settling day. We were told that, apart from the security of the deeds of both the old and the new house, we should have to get pretty heavy guarantees before a bank would lend the money. A friend suggested people who might help with the guarantee, and to one in particular she wrote herself. This elicited a luncheon invitation and we discovered that our host was the director of a bank. The outcome was that his bank agreed to negotiate the whole thing for us, and to take on the final mortgage when we had reduced it to manageable proportions. We rejoiced again, thinking that this time the house was really ours, as we had raced the auction hour and won by about three days.

Our rejoicings faded however when a friend, who was in London and in contact with things going on there, telephoned us that evening to warn us that a great deal was happening, that larger offers were being received, and that if we were not very quick we were likely to lose the property. At dawn we went up to London, and waved the deposit of £5,000 in front of the agents. They were non-committal, and refused to take the cheque, asking us to take it to our solicitors. Our solicitors took it, and telephoned immediately to make an appointment to exchange contracts early on Monday morning.

When we arrived home from London we got into touch with

the owner of the house, telling her we had paid the cheque, but she said that she was very uncertain that she would sign. Our hearts did fall this time. It seemed too much to lose it after all that had happened. When the time of the appointment to exchange contracts came, we held our breath again, and were dismayed to hear that the owner had refused to sanction her solicitors meeting ours. At that moment the manager of our new bank came by chance to see the house and was with us when the news came through. He immediately got into touch with the agents, whom he knew, and went straight back to London. The solicitors pulled all the strings they could, and another appointment was made to exchange contracts that afternoon. Finally at 2.30 that afternoon the contract was signed. We were certainly relieved, but were rather too exhausted to rejoice again with quite the same freshness as in our previous rejoicings. Now, we thought, it is certainly ours, and all that had to be done was the routine legal work, and we planned to move in the first week of January.

All went well and smoothly until we were within sight of settling day. Then a difficulty arose about a personal guarantee of £15,000 which a friend had offered at the beginning. On settling day the necessary signature had not been received. The bank refused to pay the money. The farm were in the process of moving all their livestock, equipment and themselves, and the owner, who had moved, was getting very restive. The rest of the Community were scattered at this time, as we had decided to get our annual holidays over this year before moving. Immediately we all returned. Payment was more than a fortnight overdue, and the solution not in sight. We went straight to the bank in London, and while we were there trying to find a new solution, a note was brought to us with a renewed firm offer of a guarantee. The bank agreed to pay the money in full. At last it was true, and we started to move in ourselves.

The move was made on January 19th, 1950. Ten missionaries came and helped us to move in and were quite wonderful. They scrubbed and stained floors and painted, put up curtains and did the hundred jobs we could never have done in the time at our disposal.

We have more room here, and are able to have a sitting-room for the 'workers' whom we now call 'tertiaries', and also a room for the Community. There is more space for everyone and a large library is now as far away as possible from all the house noises. The whole place is just what we needed and wanted, except for the children's house. There is however at just the right distance a farm-house. This is small, but we have plans ready to enlarge it, and if all goes well, it should be a most healthy and attractive place.

This chapter has been written just ten years after the idea was first conceived at Selly Oak. 1940-1950.

XI

THE FARM

I T W A S at Oakenrough in 1941 that the idea of animals became part of our community life. We inherited, with the house, a handful of rather elderly hens which we increased to sixteen, and they seemed to us quite a work to look after; they inhabited a hen-house at the bottom of a one hundred feet drop, so it was indeed a job to carry food and water to them.

At the same time two of our Scotties presented us with six pups, and when the time came for them to be sold we found, to our surprise, that they brought us in £40. This laid the foundation stone of our 'farm finance', and set us thinking of ways and means for earning more. We bought two goats and later on a billie, and did a small trade in kids; to them we added rabbits, and rabbits indeed became a population to themselves. They have left memories. Thomas, a little lame one, made light of an almost impossible lameness, and was such a 'person' that no one had the heart to finish his small life for him. He lived mostly in the flower garden, but did he see a pair of legs approaching from any direction, he did a kind of limping-ballet to the front of them. Everybody knew Thomas. Sometimes we put the pups in with the baby rabbits and they had fine frolics together, never seeming the least afraid of one another. The goat kids mostly inhabited the lawn and wandered in and out of the french window of the dining-room to make friends with the guests.

Someone gave us a pony, and he was our first real failure. He simply refused to be ridden, and our coats soon became full of rents and tears as he did his best to give the unwary a good bite.

When we moved to Barns Green we could not afford to take
on the farm for the first two years, and let it to the man who was
already there. We kept one field of four acres and a few loose boxes
and pig-sties and put our 'farm' in there. Some of us helped
on the farm in our spare moments and learned to milk, and in a
short time were able to give the staff time off in the week-ends by
taking over. We learned all we could from chatting with the
surrounding farmers and became more and more bitten with the
idea of one day farming in earnest as part of the Community
scheme.

One of our neighbours had two pigs, the lady rejoicing in the
name of Matilda. Matilda produced with the utmost regularity
fine litters of fifteen or sixteen piglets. One day we came home
with two of them under our arms, squealing their heads off as
though they had come to the end of all things safe in life. Then the
fun began. We needed rations for them as they grew, and approached the Ministry of Agriculture with great assurance. 'Could
we keep pigs? could we be sure of food?' 'Well', said the Ministry
of Agriculture, 'if you have a score of pigs we can give you food,
but not for two.'

There were four perfect sties, plenty of people to help, plenty of
land, and grass, everything we needed for rearing pigs and
supplying the Government's outcry for 'more pigs', but no, we
could not begin. When they were six months old we had to sell
them and begin again with two more piglets. The same applied to
chickens, we could keep only twenty-four for lack of food. The
Agriculture Committees informed us that allowances were based
on 1939 returns. There was nothing for you unless you had
started your farm in 1939. We struggled on, scrounging here and
there from friendly farmers for two years. Then one September
morning the papers announced that all rationing was cut off.
Just like that! We had managed to increase to forty hens, four
young pigs and one sow. Now we were faced with selling what
we had struggled against such odds to get.

In desperation, we set off to Chichester to see the head of the
feeding department, and we sat there repeating to his great
annoyance: 'We can't believe there is no allowance for this farm,
we feel sure there is some mistake'. Finally he was persuaded to

look up his files and to our great relief he found that we should have been having 6 cwt. of food a month all the time. We came home in great triumph and the farm increased mightily in our eyes, till by the time we made the next move to Coolham we came with fifteen milking cows, one bull, fourteen heifers, fifteen pigs, and three hundred poultry.

But that is to anticipate. In 1944 milk became terribly short. We needed it for our visitors, who were mostly from long service abroad and required good food, as also did the war-workers of England who came to us. It took *all* our courage to face the next step, but in that year we bought our first cow, a Jersey, for £20. We collected for her; one bought the head, another the tail, and so on. Before long she gave us a perfect golden calf, and never was calf so spoilt. She was like a small dog, as friendly, following us in and out.

We learned by experience what temperamental persons animals are. Some sows are good with their offspring and some are not. One never-to-be-forgotten day, Arabella turned on her babies and we had to stand over her and take them from her as they were born. To keep them warm they were brought into the kitchen, where another of us was cooking for a houseful of twenty-four. We happened to have a very interesting and talkative don in the kitchen to lunch with us that day, and the squealings of sixteen small pigs soon reduced all that was not pig to absolute silence. Another time Josephine produced the same sized litter with the same extreme annoyance over the fact, and we spent the night rescuing the young, while an officer of the B.B.C. kept us from freezing with cups of tea.

In 1945 the farmer gave up our land and returned to London, and we had to choose whether to let it to another or take it over ourselves. It *was* a choice. None of us really knew anything to speak of about farming; our spattering of knowledge had been gained from books, talks and experience only. But ninety-five acres, with real fields and ploughing to do, ditches to dig, etc., was another matter. We had no capital, and nothing to start with, not even a bucket, but we had a tremendous lot of enthusiasm, no fear of hard work, and we were longing to try. We prayed that a miracle might happen, but nothing happened. Then out of the blue a cheque for £250 came. That seemed the answer and we plunged head-foremost. We had to keep it quite separate from the house finances and stand on our own feet, as obviously we could not carry a second debt, with the mortgage on the house still to pay.

We bought a tractor for £165, made friends with the man we bought it from, and ever since he has serviced it for us, and given us all the help we needed. The brightest spot was that the farmer's foreman agreed to stay with us, pending his being able to get out to Australia. Another friend went to sales and bought for us. Several smaller gifts came, and in spite of what seemed at times to be the most crazy optimism, in October we began farming in real earnest.

The foreman was indeed a gift from heaven. He was a man of the land and an exceedingly fine gentleman. He did not seem to mind having to work with these young women who really did not know much about anything, and he was the best teacher we could have had. He never picked up our mistakes for us; he made us go back and pick them up for ourselves, which made us the more careful not to repeat that mistake. Let fifteen piglets out of the sty because you are thinking of something else and be sent to get them back by yourself, and you will not repeat that bit of carelessness. And he was unfailingly courteous even when we had done some bad bit of work, though his remarks, given in a quiet voice, nearly took the skin off us with their gentle sarcasm. One of us had been a teacher, who had never wanted to teach; one a Wren who had been offered jobs in Australia as well as in England, but who had a single-minded idea of what she wanted to do, and that was to build up a farm in community; the third, a missionary from West Africa.

We now sell milk to the Express Dairy Ltd., and supply the fifty or more people in the community guest and training house with milk, cream and eggs, an occasional table bird and a pig now and then. The cows increased to twenty-two and the machinery has now become adequate. As we look back and think how the farm has come into being bit by bit, we wonder how we ever had the audacity to start with so little. Everybody who knew had told us that you must have a capital of at least £2,000 to start with, and then you would see no returns for four years over and above expenses. There seems to be little doubt that God was helping us all the time, saving us from crashing again and again, for we never lacked for long anything that we really needed. In spite of our ignorance and mistakes, it has all gone forward, and now we have two hundred and fifty acres to look after, and endless scope ahead.

We can never adequately express our gratitude to the dozens of people who have helped us. Some have stayed for a few days and worked, and some for several weeks, and one for two years. They include students from the universities and training colleges, missionaries on furlough and in training, doctors, nurses, teachers, business men, agricultural students, Africans, and German prisoners of war. The Church Missionary Secretariat, here for conference, pulled down trees, hewed logs and helped with the harvest. During the summer months we have to put up extra tents for those who come to help with the hay-making and harvesting, and then even the older guests turn out and give a hand.

A farm can be a Christian training ground. It is a place where people must forget themselves for the sake of what is alive and needs faithful and constant attention. For those who will learn purposefully it can teach alertness, quickness, gentleness, carefulness, thoroughness, reliability, and similar virtues. You have to carry a job through whatever the weather is like or whatever you feel like.

Farming is taking the first gift of God to man and beginning with Him there, knowing that the beginning of your work must be faithfully and thoroughly done or the end will be unfruitful; and on the other hand that it is only as you do the work right through to the end that you will be able to gather fruit. It cuts out sentimentality, theorising as an end in itself, and day-dreaming of any kind. It is the beginning and the finishing of a job which makes it one, and enables you to look back and delight in a job well done. If we learn on a farm to see thought and act as one, we come to realize that in spiritual work too there must be faithful beginning and ending. We find here the explanation why many begin the Christian life so well and then suffer arrest of growth or fall into decline. Obedience to an objective demand is the only hope for the farm as it is the only hope for our life with God and His demands.

Obedience and command cannot be wiped out of the business of living; we have to see them as two sides of the same thing, an equal lifting of the thing to be done or undertaken. The right place of obedience is not primarily towards a person but outwards to the situation. I have watched two girls on the farm working a certain machine together, and there comes a time when one of them says a very peremptory 'Stop!' If the second does not obey that command, the project they are trying to bring into being fails; the one has to be as ready to obey as the other to command, but it is no arbitrary command or slavish submission, it is the action and reaction necessary for the success of the act to be brought into being as a whole and completed act. Obedience in its right place is a moment in a process, the one obeyed and the one obeying having equal parts in the same moment. In the building up of any purpose or plan, or situation within a purpose, there is a moment which we call obedience, but it leads out of all that has gone before and on to that which is being brought into being. It is a creative moment in that process and from it something that we had hoped for happens or there is a check in the process and the thing does not happen.

To work together, as we do, with different people, brings out all the usual difficulties of relationships. We have to see things together and back each other up; if we are divided in our ideas and the working of them out, the farming suffers. You can in the actual work evade for a time a difficult relationship and slip away from the distress and disagreeableness of it. But sooner or later it will trip you up, because some small need will come along and there will be disintegration instead of creation because you and some one else are not in each other's mind about it.

The farm brings home to us too in a way that cannot be forgotten our utter need of God and of reliance on Him, which we take for granted. You can feed your young heifers, keep them clean and warm, nurse them if they are ill, and that is all you can do. Only God can make them grow; you cannot. That teaches a lot about the spiritual life. You have to do all you can for your own spirit's growth, but there is a place where, whatever you do, nothing can happen without the miracle of growth. We shall get no beautiful field of golden corn next year unless we plough and weed and sow as perfectly as we know how, using the last drop of energy may be that we have in us, but we cannot do without God's part in it. On the other hand, we cannot 'leave it to God' as our innate fear and laziness would tempt us to do with the hard situation or person, unless we have done all that we can, obeying the laws of the field with all our intelligence, sensitivity to experience, and humbly taking the experience of those who know more about the subject than we do. This is a great lesson to learn. The passive among us hope that God will do it all without too much effort on our part, and the active among us try to do it all, and imagine that their efforts alone can give them the victory. The wishful thinking and expression of our own temperaments, which we imagine to be a spiritual truth, needs to be thrown into the rubbish heap of unintelligent, self-protecting opinions. The farm would be a rubbish heap very quickly if it was subject to opinions of this sort.

As we live in the fields, we find ourselves near to God, not only in loving the beauty of it all, the air and the wide freedom, but also in the delighted sense that we are creating along with Him. To be His partners in the work of creation, that is pure joy and inspiration. Our part in it is submission and humility. As we surrender to His laws, things happen, life comes. As you bend over your back-breaking task of planting out a thousand small cabbage plants, you are doing it so that He shall have the condition under which He can make it grow. Do it carelessly because you are fed-up, and 'anyhow it isn't as important as all that', and you have been the destroyer and have not collaborated with Him, who did everything and saw that it was very good.

In the farm we have a rare opportunity. In the St Julian's Community we are learning to relate thought to act, and experience in the farm confirms the lesson. We cannot make the farm submit to our passing inclinations, we have to surrender to its own complete and demanding pattern. We therefore have the chance to learn the true meaning of obedience to some demand beyond ourselves and our own emotionally driven wishes, and that is the lesson, we believe, that the world at the moment needs to learn more than almost any other lesson.

PART III

RETROSPECT AND PROSPECT

XII

FRIENDSHIP

IT WOULD be the verdict of most of those who knew Florence
Allshorn that her greatest achievement was the creative power of
her friendship. She gave herself, as Christ did, primarily to the
few; the circle of those with whom an individual, finite life
can maintain intimate intercourse can never be a wide one.
But her vitality and her power of communication were such
that she was able to maintain a rich and creative friendship with
an unusually large number of people. On those whose lives were
enriched by her friendship the mark which she left was deep and
transforming. There is a consensus of testimony from those who
enjoyed her friendship that there was in it something that was in
their experience unique.

Florence reflected much on the meaning of friendship. She
discussed it often with the other members of St Julian's Community. She wrote a paper on it which she thought might form
part of the preceding story of St Julian's written by herself. It
was left unfortunately in too unfinished a form to be used in that
way. Its contents will be combined with other material in this
chapter to interpret Florence's understanding of the meaning and
practice of friendship. A quotation from the memorandum will
provide a starting point.

We came into this adventure with the usual idea of friendship.
We could quote a lot about its ideal pattern, but we had no
idea of working for it. Mostly friendship rested on mutual
attraction and like-mindedness. That seemed all right and we
immediately drew to the one who attracted us most. But we
saw that that was not enough.

We knew well enough in theory that the love that Jesus Christ had said was to be like His own does not start like that, that it does not start with the romantic love of the poets but with the very unpoetical neighbour. There was a difference between the thing we had known as friendship and this all-embracing friendliness which Christ epitomised in His own life.

We cleared the ground as best we could by first of all asking ourselves in the light of what we were doing, what it was not. Our findings ran as follows:

It was not primarily love of the senses.

It was not a human emotion that comes for one person and not for another.

It was not an enervating sympathy, which takes away the chance of greatness from the other, and feeds her self-pity.

It is not allowing wrong in the other to go unchecked, or to be in such a state of glamour that you see no wrong in the other. It is never tolerant of evil.

It is not necessarily giving the other what she wants, being kind and indulgent.

It is not mothering; keeping the other childish and dependent.

It is not 'lovering', using the other as an emotional outlet for yourself.

None of these attitudes have the 'as I have loved you' in them; they are human, and have to be transformed by a more selfless giving, where the good of the other looms larger than your own need to give.

We agreed that we would hold back from special friend-ships in the Community until we had learned a little of this more all-embracing friendliness. We knew that the kind of friendship that wanted things for itself at any price was not the way to the thing we sought and we knew that somehow our feelings had to be trained to some new thing.

What was the real meaning of the attempt to love which the Community was making? 'Attempt to love'—how self-conscious and priggish it sounds, and yet we could love if we really saw each other—saw each other as the creation of God. Each one of us made in His image, inhabited by His Spirit, are we not lovable then? The eyes of our perception are blind, and they are culpably blind. This hypothesis that you *can* learn to see, that you *can* learn to know, means obtaining a know-ledge which will have to be as self-conscious as is the knowledge that we have to learn in order to pass an exam. We cannot love as Christ loved, but we have it in us to learn something of that love. We are thoughtless, blind and inconsiderate, but we need not be. The sum of 'all uncharitableness' in the world is an open sore. What is the alternative—to go on as we are now? Is that good enough? Which of us has 'a heart all charitable, a heart that beats sound and true with love to God and man'? To learn you must become conscious of what you do not know, and what you have to learn. And if God is in His essence love, then we are made to love as the stars are made to shine. That is why we have to be redeemed; the creation which is God's, that is ourselves, has to be redeemed because it has gone wrong.

If we are created by God and He is love, then we are love. We have lost love and we can learn to find it again. We must learn to be friendly people from the heart, not only from the social surface. This friendship will not be worth giving to one unless it is worth giving to all. That will be the difference. We shall still have our special friends, but having learnt this we shall be more worthwhile friends. There is no loss with God, only creation.

Florence's preoccupation with the question of friendship dates from many years earlier. It was the facing of this question in Uganda that was, as we have seen, the critical turning point in her life. Its far-reaching importance for the whole life and work of the Church was clearly envisaged in the article on 'The Corporate Life of a Mission Station', from which extensive quotations were made in an earlier chapter.

If we can face the situation (i.e. that which exists in the mission field) as it is [she says in that article]; if we can be interested and alarmed together, we may come to a fuller understanding and through a practical application of what we can find may build for ourselves a finer structure. The whole problem of achieving friendship lies in it, and women as a whole have not yet mastered the art of friendship between themselves. They have had no need to; the depth of their emotions has been centred in husband and children, and where they have not found that outlet they have too seldom learned what to do with these emotions. They have the instinct to possess and fight for their own, they have the perfectly natural possessive, jealous and mothering instinct. These instincts do not melt away naturally if a woman is not married. We have to recognize them in ourselves and deal with them by lifting them on to a higher and more selfless plane. The values of a close relationship, the daily companionship, the shared life interest in a home—in working out these lies to a great extent our sanctification. And if we are forced to work them out with someone from whom we are temperamentally different, then if we can set out on it together the adventure is larger, there are deeper levels to be touched and the chance of a finer victory.

Our pitfalls lie in these unsanctified natural instincts, which create such an attitude as, for example, seeing the new recruit as 'someone to help me in the job', or (less conscious perhaps) 'someone on whom I can lavish my mothering instinct', while we fail to realize that the Christlike thing is not to use any person to satisfy ourselves, but to see that she goes free of us and our requirements and self-expression.

What is said in this quotation about the needs of unmarried women has its roots in clear and deeply considered convictions which Florence had reached on the subject of marriage. In her view marriage, like all other conditions in life, was a circumstance, and the thing that mattered, as she always insisted, was what you did with your circumstances. If you were married, you had one set of joys, opportunities and problems and, if you were unmarried, you had another set. Florence believed that life could be lived fully in either set of circumstances. She denied vehemently that women who were not married necessarily suffered from frustration. She saw many instances of frustration in married life as well as among single women. If people refused the way of 'self-naughting' and of love, as Florence understood love, they could meet with frustration in both the married and the unmarried state, while if they chose the way of love they could find victory and happiness in either.

For herself she chose freedom from the ties of family life. She never felt that she had missed something in life by remaining unmarried. 'Joan of Arc', she writes, 'was my ideal—she and Florence Nightingale—when I was about twenty, and the single-minded, lonely thing will always be for me the ideal, but isn't it a mercy that we aren't all alike?' Others might choose differently, and marriage was an equally worthy choice and equally rich in possibilities.

In the discussion which followed the last address which she ever gave she was asked whether marriage was a hindrance to work for the Kingdom of God and gave this reply:

> I don't think it makes any difference whether you are married or unmarried. Whether you are married or unmarried is a circumstance within the Christian life. If you are married, you have a special task, if you are unmarried you have something else to do. Both have a different witness to give. I think the married home can be one of the greatest witnesses you can make these days, because there are so many unhappy marriages, so much misery. In being married you can redeem the word marriage and make it something beautiful again. On the other hand, I think the unmarried person has something very fine to do, in showing that without having anything the world says you must have if you are going to be happy, you can still be happy and fulfilled, and I am very glad I have been able to prove that true. I had no parents since the age of three. I never had any money, never had any future, I tried to be an artist and couldn't, I never had husband or children, yet I am as happy as anybody I know. I am really fulfilled. So I do not think it matters.

For Florence friendship was never simply the relation of two persons to one another; it was always rooted in a deeper reality. She was one of the 'thrice blest . . . whose loves in higher love endure'. Nothing was more characteristic of her than the power to see life steadily in its true proportions. First things with her were really first. Seeing God was the central reality of her life. Friendship consequently was for her the relation of two persons whose eyes are fixed on God's will and purpose and whose hearts are unceasingly open to the love which He freely squanders on all His children. These are Christian commonplaces. It was the intensity with which Florence apprehended them and the richness of the content that they had for her that gave to her life a peculiar quality.

Since true friendship is based, not on two people looking at and appreciating one another, but on both looking outside themselves and pursuing the same goal, friendship is possible even between persons who were naturally incompatible, or even antipathetic to one another. 'If you are both looking at Jesus Christ', she used to say, 'you can't *not* meet.' 'At roots you do see positively', she writes to a friend, 'that God is in every one and that we can't really be contemptuous and hateful when we approach ground where God dwells.' And again, 'I can't dislike people; I take Jesus Christ too seriously.' And in another letter, 'I learn so much from the people I can't like. Every bit of Christ's love I can get hold of enables me to see more.' Friendship with Florence meant, as one of her younger friends discovered, 'going on the same road as she was going'.

Love for Florence was not a duty but a passion. It was the end, and the glory of life. 'We are all playing', she writes in a letter, 'or trying to play a symphony to God. Sometimes I feel I'd do anything, give anything away, if it would help some one to play right.' And in another letter, appealing to an old student to help one of her fellow-missionaries: 'Oh, B——, *anything* is worth while to get the unhappiness out of life. Hear the trumpets blowing, when you're tempted to take the line of least resistance.'

Already in her Sheffield days, as we can see from the extracts from her letters quoted in the first chapter, she was aware of a distinction, and of a possible conflict, between natural and spiritual love. But while the difference became increasingly clear to her, the two were never allowed to fall apart. It was always the whole person that she loved.

What she desired most for her friends was the complete fulfilment of their being. One who was much younger than she was and who knew her only for a relatively short period in her last years writes:

> More than all else, of course, I was conscious that she saw us all as the people we were meant to be. This sounds so easy, but I think it is one of the rarest and most difficult things in the world. I have never known anyone else who so consistently saw other people as God meant them to be, whole, free, generous, compassionate, loving human beings. It was this discernment in her that must have made life, for those close to

her (and here I am guessing, for I was not one of them), an
agony as well as a joy, an adventure that taxed all the resources
of the spirit, an affair for the valiant hearted only. For seeing
people as they were meant to be implies seeing them, a hundred
times a day perhaps, as they are. And against that discrepancy
she could wage a holy war indeed. She knew the pain involved
for most people in trying to get free from self, free from the
crippling bandages of pride, of doing the right things from the
wrong motives, and all the subterfuges behind which we
entrench ourselves. Against all these she struggled passionately,
seeking to cut through their strangleholds and to liberate the
essential, the real, person within. Do you remember the Button
Moulder in *Peer Gynt*, and how, in that tragic last act he says to
Peer when he meets him at the end of his vainglory, 'You were
meant for a shining button on the waistcoat of the world; but
your loop got broken'? Florence herself understood magni-
ficently about shining buttons and broken loops; and, like the
Button Moulder, she knew that sometimes there was no remedy
short of a complete 'recasting'. But all the time she saw men
and women shining in their original image through and
beyond the dust and the tarnish that, for most of us, make up
the greater part of our lives.

What Florence saw in people she once described in a letter:

It's keeping your eye on that secret thing. I know it in animals
and flowers. Each does take on a warm, small, secret personality if you've time to *look*. Whether it's a pup or a violet they
are themselves, and even when the pup has just torn up my new
bag, it's still there—a sort of innocent warmth, a secrecy,
something beyond me. And that's the fundamental quality of
persons too. That is what makes you long to help to twist the
little distorted bit straight, because in the end it will twist the
whole. I think I've always seen this, but it's become so much
clearer. It's the job of helping God to bring that secret, remote
beauty to the outside, instead of these more shallow nicenesses
and fitful goods.

Love in the eyes of Florence was real love only in so far as it
was redeeming love. She could not see one whom she loved in the
grip of anything evil without exerting all her power to set her
free. To shut one's eyes to the evil, to seek some easy adjustment,

to settle down to a comfortable working relationship was weakness and cowardice. It was to allow something rich and triumphant to go out of life.

A 'weak and unreal surface pleasantness' was something that Florence could not abide. There was no solid and assured basis of friendship except *truth*. To be afraid of being hurt in the attempt to redeem another was a betrayal of truth. The purpose of the St Julian's Community was 'to build one another up in the truth'.

Florence would often express her own deepest convictions in a quotation from some other writer. 'Life', she quotes, 'is perpetual decision—it must be. It is not some smooth adjustment we can hope to achieve once for all and then coast along with. It is rather a constant achievement in the teeth of forces which tear us apart'. That was Florence's conception of friendship.

Her sense of the sternness and severity of love deepened as the years passed. This was noticeable in her relations with those who were closest to her. In the days when she was training students her great gift seemed to be to bring out the best in them. She would write to them 'All my thoughts of you are happy ones,' and tell them how much she believed in them and expected from them. Cheered by this confidence they were ready to do anything for her.

For herself, to see a truth was to integrate it with the rest of her life. But she found that with others this was not always so. Assent to a truth did not mean that it would be translated into act. She was sometimes a long time in making this discovery, even in the case of those who were most intimately associated with her. She seemed sometimes to go almost to the other extreme. She realized that her earlier way of helping people did not always get down to the root of the evil in them. She became increasingly sensitive to evil. She saw the injury it did to people by keeping them back from the lovely kingdom in which life was meant to be lived. In place of the beautiful, exciting things she had been wont to say she would use hard and withering language. Her tone became sterner. She realized the cost of this; it made it more difficult to 'enjoy' people and take delight in them in the way she had done. She could write to one of her closest friends such a note as this:

Ruskin says, 'You will find on really looking honestly that your mind is little better than a rough wilderness, neglected and stubborn, partly barren, partly overgrown with pestilent bushes and venomous wind-sown herbiage of evil surmise, and the first thing to do is *eagerly and scornfully* to set fire to this, burn all the jungle into wholesome ash heaps and then plough and sow.' I've been trying to do this for you because you wouldn't do it for yourself—so you must believe that all the furious hard things I've said have only been me taking a rake and trying to get rid of the rubbish for you.

You must *see* straight—or else the adventure of you with me is a catastrophe of the first water. I have been eager and scornful for you because you wouldn't be eager and scornful for yourself, and my banging and calling you the worst names I could think of somehow to *get through* has been much saner and cleaner than your self-pity and resentment and boggy remembrances. So start and be eager and scornful, not depressed and downed—and be thankful someone is eager and scornful for you.

Or again:

The reason why you don't learn quickly is because your first reaction is to *justify* yourself. This is always the place where I get angry with you. We go in entirely different directions here and I too am losing my patience with you. If you don't *hate* your justifications like poison you'll always dribble into things or drift out of them. But there is a truth to be faced and it hasn't to be made to fit into what you are like. You have to toe up to it. Either you re-orientate your seeing or we go different paths.

But she was, at the same time, very quick to change her whole attitude as soon as she saw in the one she was attacking any stirring of humility or of grace. Those with her could never be certain what at any given time her keen and penetrating eyes were seeing. One of those nearest to her, whom she dearly loved, confesses that she was never entirely free from a certain fear of Florence, which never diminished in the slightest degree her intense love for her. In Jesus Christ there was the same strain of austerity. In His case also the disciples, as they followed, were afraid.

One would have supposed that living in community would have been in comparison with some tasks relatively easy. The atmosphere in which visitors to St Julian's found themselves was one of peace, happiness and quiet efficiency. But the reign of harmony and calm, which visitors found so restful, was not a natural beauty on which they had chanced to light, but a hardly won creative achievement.

It was not merely because she felt that she had given most of what she had to give in the sphere of missionary training that Florence turned aside from that work and embarked on the St Julian's experiment, but because she felt the need for a new intensive, more direct attack on the evil that kept professing Christians in fetters and held them back from the liberty that was theirs.

There is a revealing sentence in one of Florence's circular letters written after five years experience of the St Julian's adventure. 'The devil', she writes, 'is certainly as anxious to get into St Julian's and do his wrecking as anywhere I have been, but there is a good fight against him here, and we have learned a lot since we started this venture. It has been quite the stiffest bit of my life, but lovely too.' 'Quite the stiffest bit of my life' from Florence means a great deal, and the addition of 'but lovely too' is highly characteristic. She looked on the St Julian's venture as an opportunity of becoming 'more real' and that was the hardest task of all.

> Here in St Julian's [she said in one of her talks] one comes into a community of persons intent on finding the secret of true wholeness of living and their right relation to the transcendent Spirit. At first this may appear to be an easy friendly road, but once it is entered upon fully it is the sternest and most disturbing challenge to one's unreal, so often shallow, and usually mediocre attempts at Christianity.

The closer and more continuous relations of community showed how deep-seated and stubborn were the roots of evil. The fight against it acquired a new intensity. Florence did not shrink from the battle. It is the saint who perceives the devil, and when the power of evil manifested itself in the community life Florence took the brunt upon herself. She allowed herself to be caught in its web. She stood by the side of the other and shared in the struggle, though to her pure spirit the involvement in evil was at times almost unbearable. She would do this, if need be, day in and day out, because she would accept no lower standard than to love as Jesus loved. But the cost to her, when she was longing to stretch her wings in the ascent to God, cannot be measured. That is the unanimous testimony of those who were her fellow-members in the Community.

None of those who were close to Florence ever doubted that whatever there was in her of austerity and severity was itself the expression of an intense love. The same letter that contains a confession of a certain fear of her asserts that 'her sympathy was quite indescribable'. That her sternness was the manifestation and not the betrayal of love was made clear to all by two things.

The first was that all her sternness was directed in the first instance relentlessly against herself. Her attack on evil in another proceeded from a singular selflessness. 'Love like hers', writes one who was very close to her, 'is very, very rare. She never wanted *anything* from *anyone* for herself. She only wanted the other person to be with Jesus Christ, to know Him, and she would do anything to make that possible.'

The humility which underlay all that Florence did is revealed in the following passage in one of her letters:

I think that the only difference between me and you younger ones is this. I am more conscious when I am playing the Pharisee than you are. You have to be very much aware of that. The clearer the capacity for seeing, the greater danger of playing the Pharisee. We are all *equal* in sin. I am very sure of that. I *know* it and when you come away from a talk with anyone and feel you are righter than she is, look out. If I tell someone something unpleasant I come away with a real humble wonder that she hasn't kicked me out. Me with a beam in my eye getting out the mote too. And this business of telling each other what is wrong is so important and so deadly danger-ous it is the most awful sin unless you go straight to God and ask for His forgiveness for your own and feel a real gratitude and reverence towards the other.

In another letter she writes:

You still have to learn how to give the truth. If you depress a person with it, you have given it without Christ's love constraining you, and without His patience, and you won't lift. It's grand work, but hard. And remember there's a damned lot of the Pharisee in us all and we have to have that despair about it which hurls us back on the forgiveness of God and our own utter blightedness.

And on another occasion:

I see that you are getting freer from yourself all the time. The things that are wrong in ourselves are so stupid, and I do get impatient with them both in myself and in my friends, don't you? If I hammer so unmercifully it's because I really *feel* feelings are *not* important—truth is—and I feel I don't want to think of them. I want to honour my friend enough to believe she doesn't give a hoot for her feelings either. They are so little to the point. If I go too hard at you, it's because I see it like that. All the richness and beauty of your nature must get free so that it flows purely. And we are both having the same adventure. I feel a worm these days. I can't tell you, but also I feel a gladness because I have my eyes set on Christ and I know Him in me. *That's* what matters.

The self-discipline to which Florence submitted herself for the sake of others is revealed in the following passage from a letter in the days when she was engaged in training:

I have a great horror of plunging deep into personality, we all have so much of the primeval slime at the bottom of us and it's safer and happier to live with the better part of it and shut your eyes to the worse. But it won't get anywhere. I've got to learn root causes for failure and I shan't do it if I stand in a sort of crow's nest out of it all. I'll have to go down and it won't be only going down into the grim darkness of other people, but of myself as well. I can foresee that dimly. If I stir up slime-covered roots in others, the evil miasma must stir up slime-covered roots in me too. But if in so doing we could cleanse our roots—jealousies, resentments, prides—that would be most worthwhile.

It was the fact that Florence had achieved self conquest and a rare disinterestedness that enabled her to deal searchingly with the evil in others. Those whom she trained as missionaries, or to whom she gave further training at St Julian's, were able to see with varying degrees of understanding what she was trying to do. But not all were able to assimilate it fully, and few had passed through the experiences of suffering by which the truth had entered into the fibres of her being. They were in danger of imitating her methods before having proved on their own pulses the reality of her experience.

It could not but happen to her, what has happened to all great teachers, that many disciples pick up and repeat their language, and to some extent their ideas, without having made the substance their own. This danger was peculiarly great in regard to the truths which Florence sought to inculcate, since it belonged to the nature of these truths that their meaning could be grasped and communicated only in living them. Some of those trained by her, when they reached the mission field, failed to exhibit the wisdom and tact which the situation demanded. Too often they were tempted to quote St Julian's as a final spiritual authority, and sometimes even to justify their own inexpert handling of a situation by saying that they were practising what they had learned at St Julian's. It does not need any great experience of life to see that such attitudes were likely to give rise to misunderstanding and antagonism, particularly between younger and more senior missionaries, i.e. to produce precisely the thing which it was the primary concern of Florence to overcome. But these criticisms, which not infrequently were directed against St Julian's, are justifiable criticisms not of Florence's insights and practice, but of misunderstandings and distortions of her teaching and methods.

Florence was able to distinguish clearly between spiritual evil and what was due to natural temperament and disposition. She says, for example, in a letter:

M—— has every right to be what you see as slow and dull if that is her way of expressing herself. It may be warped but there it is and you throw yourself up against a stone wall when you fret against it because it frustrates your own self-expression. Sometimes I think we people with ideas are selfish. We go so fast we never see whether our ideas are wanted or heeded at the moment, or whether a slower thing may not help just as much. Our self-expression is in ideas so much and we blame because people won't move fast enough to carry them out for us or with us. So often, though, when we have flung ourselves about with our ideas, and fumed and fretted, when in the end we get quiet again we find that the slow people have steadfastly and faithfully carried on with the simple true things. It all seems such a muddle, but I am sure too that every impatience of a quick mind only makes a slow one withdraw into a more obstinate and sad dullness, if it's that kind of slow mind.

And again:

Accept fussiness. Say to yourself, 'Well it's just as important for her to fuss as it is for me to read.' You can get right out of the reach of its power over you, if you accept it. Try to grip what I mean. We all express ourselves differently. It's her way of expressing herself. Say to yourself, 'Well, hang it, why shouldn't she fuss if she wants to—why should she do what I want?'

The second thing that made it possible for Florence Allshorn to deal searchingly with the faults and weaknesses in her friends was that her doing this was so obviously an expression of an intense love for the entire person. 'She knew you', writes one of her closest friends, 'to the depths of your rotten roots, and also yet still *loved* you.' 'When I get at you again and again', she writes to a fellow-member of the Community, 'try to believe that it is because I see what you could be, and that I have my arm round you, even when I am striking at that thing in you.' And another recalls that she went to Florence to get her advice about a difficult decision, and that the latter's unhesitating judgment was that the hard course must be chosen. 'You must', she said, 'or you will betray the truth—you *must*.' But there were tears in Florence's eyes, and the other knew that she had not to face the hard duty alone.

The intensity of her love for her friends is revealed in the following letter:

I would go and be shut up in a tiny prison and have bread and water for years till *you were free* out in the gay sunny places, if I could. Why won't God let us do things for each other? I really would, and that's one further than being willing to die for your friend. I would do it so gladly. All I can do is preach. But oh! I get filled with such a wild and unbearable regret when I see people spoiling what is so lovely—life as it's meant to be, when people are too happy to take offence, too *keen* on beauty to bear an ugliness in another or go ugly themselves. It's worth conquering all along the line—attitudes of positive *love* always in every tiny thing. Practise, practise, practise as you would if you were Paderewski.

Not only was Florence's severity combined with a great tenderness, but her attack on evil in another always took place in the totality of her relation to that other. She loved in her friend not only the person that she was meant to be, but the person that she actually was. Even when she was attacking, the wealth of her human love for her friends was the unchanging background.

She was unstinting in the care and tenderness which she lavished on those around her. She took a delight in giving. Anything belonging to her that she felt that another needed or would like to have she gave away with both hands and without a moment's thought—clothes, fruit, sweets, little things bought on shopping expeditions, things that she had made herself. The experience of those who lived with her at St Julian's finds an echo in a letter written from East Africa about the visit she paid to Kenya and Uganda within two years of her death.

Her pleasure in the things people had given her, and specially in the things they had made for her journey; and her equal pleasure in giving things away. East Africa must be strewn with the clothes, books, bags, hats, belts, that she would give us with a quick 'This would be good for you: I don't want it now.' She loved any beautiful or well made thing, and it was so delightful to find something for her that she must have had many possessions, but few of them stayed with her for long. She travelled light.

A member of the Community relates how on one occasion Florence asked her to take charge of two baby puppies that needed to be fed during the night. When she went to her room she found

I

a glorious fire burning in the grate, a beautiful vase of flowers, a poem by Florence herself and a slab of chocolate. She realized with a pang how untidy she had herself left the fireplace, and that Florence had cleaned up the grate and fetched the sticks and coal with which to light the fire.

Throughout Florence's life her letters were full of such sentences as these. 'If you will come here [i.e. to her cottage at Mundesley] I will make your room lovely.' 'I wish I had something lovely I could send you from here. I wish I could send you the wind blowing down the grass and its rising so gaily afterwards, and lovely hay-y smells and sea-weedy smells and all the clear, clean coolness—not much sun, but so much clearness. You love that.'

She knew that her friends had natural human, as well as spiritual, needs. The following passage in one of her letters is characteristic:

Do you have your free day away from them entirely? I wish you would go under holy obedience and go up to town and go to a theatre or cinema each week. Now I am going to suggest something. Will you come down here for next Monday night and then come up to town and I'll take you into the world. You are sitting there and trying to be too good. I do not think it is the best thing at all. It will only mean being away one night, and we can have a talk as well. Do try.

Here is another passage of unconscious self-revelation.

A lovely bit I found in an old *Times*:

Upon the bread and salt of Russia bred,
His heart with her high sorrow soared and bled.
He kept the bitter bread and gave away
The shining salt to all who came his way.

What a gay, courageous pure way of living—let's hate the bitterness and never, never, never give it to any one.

XIII

THE PERSON SHE WAS

H O W I S I T possible to imprison Florence Allshorn in a book?
What hope is there of being able to recapture the vivid and
pulsating life which we knew, the succession of unexpected
flashes that never ceased to surprise? Yet, the attempt to portray
her in this and the following chapter, even though it can consist of
no more than hints and pointers, may yet contribute something
to an understanding of what she was. It is sometimes only when
a life has reached its close that it is seen in retrospect in its full
significance and true proportions. When it has run its full course
and can be envisaged as a whole, what Shakespeare calls its 'idea',
its essential meaning, may stand out with a new clarity.

> *The idea of her life shall sweetly creep*
> *Into his study of imagination;*
> *And every lovely organ of her life*
> *Shall come apparell'd in more precious habit,*
> *More moving—delicate and full of life*
> *Into the eye and prospect of his soul,*
> *Than when she lived indeed.*

The word 'life' recurs four times in these few lines, thrice as a
noun and once as a verb. It is the word that comes first into the
mind when one thinks of Florence Allshorn. She had an insati-
able zest for life. It was for her a many-coloured flame, the lights
and shades of which were to be loved and enjoyed on the instant,
since every second brought an experience that would never be
repeated. In almost any company she was distinguished by an
outshining vitality. She herself recognized, in one of the very few

entries in a private journal which she kept very intermittently, that she had perhaps 'a little more alertness all round than most of the people I live amongst.' Some of her friends would put it more strongly. 'When she was present', writes one, 'she made the rest of us look half dead.'

She had a passion for beauty, order and creation. The world for her was 'charged with the grandeur of God.' It was His creation, and she took endless delight in its manifold revelation of beauty and in being the partner of God in the work of perfecting it. Both in the house and in the garden she never tired of creating beauty. Her sensitive awareness could be seen in her choice of clothes, in her arrangement of a room or of a tiny vase of flowers, in her love of pictures and books, of fine leather and hand-stamped papers, of fine embroidery, of a well-ironed tray-cloth, a clean scrubbed table or a polished floor, of a carefully arranged dinner table, of a well-written letter, or of crisp overalls. 'All of us', writes one of her friends, 'saw how ceaseless her questing was, whether for that one perfect rose that transformed the flowers in the chapel, or for the placing of a picture to catch the light. She rejoiced in such signal triumphs over the ugly or the merely utilitarian.' And another writes: 'She transformed what was commonplace to most of us into a breathless adventure. It was exciting to arrange chairs in a sitting-room with her, or saucepans in a kitchen, or to build a new rabbit-hutch. Each detail held its significance because of its place in a larger vision—*to love into beauty* whatever she met, whether it was a soul or a material object.'

Her love of beauty and order made her intolerant of everything that was shoddy and second-rate. The dull, the drab, and the mediocre revolted her. Such things seemed to her a denial of the good and perfect will of God. In every sphere of life she sought what was excellent. Nothing less than the highest standard would satisfy her. Her attitude to clothes was indicative of much else about her—her dislike of all that was untidy and slovenly. 'Attractiveness is freshness', she would quote; 'it means being fastidiously clean, of course, but it means more. It means looking tubbed, brushed and finished, never obviously in need of a manicure or shampoo. It means crisp, clean clothes.' 'How can you go to the prayer room', she would ask, 'and leave a sink like that?'

She was grieved when she saw others neglecting opportunities of creating beauty. 'I find it hard to forgive A.,' she writes, 'for not loving this house into beauty.' In her visit to East Africa shortly before the close of her life she was distressed to find mission-stations which might have worn a quite different look if those in charge of them had had a flair for landscape gardening and trained eyes to see a *whole*. 'If you don't see a whole why be quite so satisfied about it? Even after seeing the next station, which is thought out and lovely, they can be satisfied to go on muddling the place up.'

She felt in herself a constant urge to bring a thing into being —to give it form. Everything one did might be putting a bit of love into the house, an act of creating in place of defiling or destroying. She was fond of quoting Rilke that 'the whole of life must pass through the hand of the sculptor into stone.' 'I always know', she would often say, 'who has done this room; some of you just do a room, others get the touch and feel of it.' She used to say with reference to a thought or an ideal: 'It is not yours, until it has come out of your finger tips.'

The creative attitude to life determined her whole outlook. 'Christianity', she would constantly say, 'is to-day and to-morrow; the past is only material.' She was impatient with yesterday. She would not allow the mistakes and flaws of yesterday to spoil to-day and to-morrow. Mistakes had no importance for her except as a place of new learning. 'It's what you do with your experiences', she always insisted, 'that matters.'

She took constant delight in the beauty of words and the vivid phrase. 'I am sure your language does get more vivid through receiving the Spirit,' she wrote to a colleague. 'It gives you a greater awareness of seeing, so that you collect vivid words. I do that consciously. Whenever I see a vivid adjective or phrase, I copy it into a book, but phrases swim into my head from nowhere too, and I recall vivid words unconsciously.' She had a constant urge to express her thoughts in poetry, and made repeated attempts to find the word or the line that would satisfy her, but her life did not leave her leisure to publish anything.

Her delight in the created world made her a great lover of

animals. No picture of Florence would be complete which left
out her animal friends. The Community at St Julian's included a
large number of them—Scotch terriers, kittens, livestock of all
kinds, the pony Jock and the donkey Marcus. Small, helpless
animals made a strong appeal to her and would settle contentedly
in her hands, knowing themselves to be safe there. The piteous
crying of a lamb would send her searching everywhere till she had
restored it to its mother.

The birds are absurdly busy all over this garden [she writes in a
letter]. At present I am specially fascinated with one grey
speckly horse which flies to the gate when I call it, one ginger
cat which sits and sees things I don't, one wicked pup which
lives in a whirl of wrong-doing, one blue tit and one robin.
Animals are *the* most restful things.

In the days when she was at St Andrew's she had a Sealyham
terrier. The following extracts from letters reveal her feelings
towards him.

The only males in this establishment are the gardener, who is
fifty odd, and Peter (my dog). Peter has become very possessive, he wouldn't let the maid make my bed this morning till
I went up and dragged him off by main force. He retaliated
by eating a fair-sized portion of Findlay's *Acts of the Apostles*
while I wasn't looking! I suppose he had a right to be mad
because after all I never did thank him for being so loyal about
my bed.

And, as if I hadn't enough with all that, here's Peter being
brought to me by an outraged housemaid with the hem of her
dress hanging round her legs. I *do* sympathise with Peter, it
must be wonderful to go berserk suddenly and tear your
nearest bit of the world to bits, what a mad exulting moment,
worth paying for.

Peter ate half a pound of lovely chocolates J. gave me and
wasn't sick! I do think he's a super-dog.

When Florence visited East Africa towards the close of her life
she was taken to see a temporary zoo where captured animals

were kept to be sent later to zoos in all parts of the world. The man in charge was away, but the visitors were taken round by his four small sons.

We went to see the obvious favourites [writes a friend who accompanied her], the cheetahs, and four small boys and four cheetahs tumbled happily over each other in an inextricable muddle. But the next cage was of leopards. 'You can never tame a leopard', they told us. 'Daddy says it's the one animal you can't tame.' The terrified and terrifying creatures certainly gave that impression as they leapt and crashed again and again at the bars in a frenzy of desire to tear us limb from limb. I winced at every leap, but Florence stood quite still, and in the car going home she said, 'I wouldn't want to rest until I had tamed those leopards.'

Mention has been made of Florence's astonishing vitality. She was always ready to volunteer to do any extra or not very pleasant job in the house. If another member of the Community or some one assisting in the house was late with her work, or had a particularly busy day before her, Florence would be quick to notice it, and would come and ask whether she might do the potatoes or whatever else needed to be done, though her own day was already full of things which to the person she was ready to help seemed of much greater importance. Her abounding vitality communicated itself to others. A passing word on the pathway, and still more a talk, would send the other person away with a new stimulus to pour her energies into some creative task.

Florence's intellectual gifts were not outstanding, but she had a good and quick mind. An able graduate student who was sent to her for training at Kennaway Hall was impressed by the quality of her lectures, which seemed to her in no way to fall short of university standards. Florence's reading was wide in range and large in quantity. The library at St Julian's, which is one of its remarkable features, and which includes a large proportion of the more important books on subjects of general interest published in recent years, was in the main her creation. Buying books was one of her special enjoyments and she was guided in her choice by an almost unerring instinct. She loved the poets and had read nearly all the two or three hundred volumes on the poetry shelves in the library. She read novels with avidity, sometimes two a week. She was fond of biography and missed few of the important publications in this field. She kept abreast of modern thought on a variety of subjects. She particularly enjoyed books that stretched her mind. She was well-read in theology, but inclined more to books on the Person of Jesus and about St Paul than to works of dogmatic theology. But above all the Bible was her meat and drink. She never tired of it, and drew inspiration from it to the end of her life.

She had in her Storrington days commented on the relation of reading to growth.

Only pain makes you grow. So does reading strong stuff, but it has to be strong. Even rotten, bad, strong stuff is better than milk-and-watery stuff, if you have got your foundations right.

She had good administrative gifts. One of them was the capacity to devolve responsibility, and she left the business side of things for the most part to others. But when big decisions had to be taken, as, for example, in the purchase of the houses at Barns Green and Coolham, she took the lead with a faith, energy and shrewdness of judgment second to none.

But her supreme gift was the artist's gift of *seeing*. It is the word that recurs most often in her letters and talks.

The world being the wonderful thing it is, the first necessity is that it should be *seen*. Like Fra Lippo Lippi in Browning's poem, Florence wanted to know what the world which God had made was *for*. Was it

> To be passed over, despised? Or dwelt upon,
> Wondered at?

But to be wondered at, it must first be seen as it really is.

'Never stop asking to be made to see', she continually urged upon her students. 'Seeing', she would say, 'is the biggest thing in the world.'

A prophet of the day has said that the modern European has forgotten how to *see*; he can only think.

The country is so incredible. I just go out and stare at it and sit in it and walk in it and listen to it. It's full to the brim, and there is not half enough time to catch what it says.

It's always 'seeing' something that gets you on—really seeing. You seeing yourself as Scott pioneering—four men shut into one hut for months with nothing to do, waiting till the winter broke, never a word of complaint about the conditions; if your soul were *seeing* that spirit of uncomplainingness, because of the huge hope of what we were meant to achieve.

It was Florence's constant aim with those whom she was training to get them to *look* at things—to look at a tree or a picture till it yielded up its meaning, to look every day for a week at the horse in the next field in order to be able to see it as it really was. 'Don't say that', she would exclaim; '*look at it.*'

The same need for seeing lay at the root of her view of relations between persons. 'When some one is talking, you have to see *her*—not what she's saying but what she *is*, and you can't do that if you're behind your own buttons. You have to be outside yourself, forget yourself.' 'What frightens me', she writes to a colleague about some one who talked piously and persuasively and had in a prolonged stay in St Julian's shown herself to possess a strong self-will and an inability to learn from any one else, 'is the way you take what people *say*. It's no use doing that unless you are aware of what lies behind the words.'

'People are so lovable', she wrote, 'when you see all of them.'

One of her notable characteristics was a childlikeness that never left her. References to this recur frequently in the letters about her. A member of the Community writes for example:

Even to the end she delighted in a day 'off' in London, in the morning coffee in some nice shop, in the after-lunch cigarette, in the excitement of someone ringing up saying 'come for a drive with me this afternoon', which was unexpected. Sometimes after a heavy week she used to say 'Let's go out in the car,' and we would trundle off. (It was in this way that we found St Julian's, Coolham.) She loved holidays and exploring new places, and found so many things to be 'bliss'. It was 'bliss' to get into bed after evening prayers and read a novel, and be given a cup of tea.

Florence had an irrepressible sense of fun. Abundant illustrations might be given, but one must suffice.

There was a Christmas party once [writes a friend] when she insisted that the whole company—very shy of each other, and including a bishop, an African girl, a young German prisoner-of-war and many homeless people—should play a racing game which consisted in sending an empty match-box cover along contesting lines of people by means of passing it from one nose to the next. Florence herself was good at this, having been blessed with a fine, aquiline variety of nose, but was reduced to helpless laughter in her efforts to pass the match-box on to the African girl next to her, whose nose seemed not so specially designed for the game. I saw them later, in a corner, gravely measuring each other's nose in order to see just why it had been so difficult.

One whose eyes and mind were so open to the wonder and variety of the world, and whose response to whatever engaged her attention in the living present was so whole-hearted and ardent, was bound at times to seem puzzling to her friends. Life for Florence was too illimitable and rich to be comprehended in any consistent and tidy pattern.

She was a creature of paradoxes [writes one friend] that alternately shocked and delighted—practical and visionary, sparkling and austere, quicksilver and serene. I have seen her hold a supper-table in fits of laughter, and I have seen her enter the dark places of a soul with the gift of peace. Intense love of beauty and the arts went hand in hand with a realism that was almost ruthless. One had to be ready for anything—the sophisticated, the Bohemian, the madcap, the stern, the gentle, the gay—everything turn about, except the dull and the conventional.

'She had a glorious understanding of paradox', says a friend who was close to her throughout the whole of the St Julian's experiment, 'as it worked out in daily life, as well as in dogma. I had no understanding of paradox—to me it was pure and simple contradiction. I went through agonies trying to understand her, when she seemed so impossibly contradictory.'

She had no wish to be thought consistent. She knew that in a constantly changing world consistency was impossible. If a previous statement by her was quoted against her, she would reply, 'But that was yesterday.' What she had been seeing then might be quite different from what she was seeing now.

What we have been mainly concerned with in the present chapter has been her natural disposition and endowment. But she was in an exceptional sense a *whole* person. In her in an unusual degree faith, thought and being were one. Her mind, her seeing, her feeling, even her physical constitution were all subject to the permeating and transforming influence of her communion with the unseen world. In the description that has been given of what was natural and individual in her, evidences of the transfiguring power of grace have everywhere crept in. We must turn now to the faith by which her whole life was directed and controlled.

XIV

HER VISION OF LIFE

UNDERLYING the manifoldness of Florence's responses to an ever-changing reality was an unswerving singleness of aim. What gave to her life the quality of greatness is that it can justly be said of her that she saw life steadily and saw it whole. She distinguished with singular consistency between the essential and the secondary. She had been given by nature a finely proportioned body; the life which her spirit fashioned was conspicuous for the balance, symmetry and splendour of its proportions.

Nature, in which Florence took endless delight, was to her the revelation of the divine beauty. The people in whom she saw infinite possibilities were persons created by God and intended by Him for a glorious fulfilment. God was to her in actual experience the supreme reality. She used to say that when she was young she would put peas in her shoes to help her to remember God. One who knew her only in the last years of her life says,

> She seems to me consistently to have said Yes to God, and therefore to life. For Florence's answer was never the pious answer that so many of us give, that self-conscious obedience that seems so often to take the colour out of life. Her assent, her obedience, put the colour into life, and in so doing she enabled others to see a new world, informed by beauty and light.

> There is only one test of our prayer life really [she writes to a friend]—are we wanting God? Do we want Him so much that we will go on if it takes five, six, ten years to find Him with that steady determination not to let up till we do—a *determination* that even goes on when there seems no success at all?

The primary object of prayer is to know God better—we and our needs should be second.

We cannot get down to the deep inner source of ourselves where the secret sins and goodnesses lie, the place we call the soul, but that is the only place He deals with, not the marginal self where we mostly live. I do not want circumstances to be better, I want you to get on top—to stretch big—that's the *only* way.

And in another letter:

Keep just looking at God, not at people. That's the solution— to have a pure capacity for God. . . . I wish I could send some beauty to you. Keep hold, the most beautiful thing in all the world is with you—God.

I think it is true to say that there are few days when we are able to look up and say, 'It has been a wonderful day with *you*'. Most often it is the job and the people and the reactions to both that fill our tired minds at the end of the day.

Talking of the practice of the presence of God, Florence says:

The only way I can learn it is to do it, and one thing I am very sure of for myself is that to sit quietly before God doing nothing, only fixing the will gently on some expressive word like 'O God, I want Thee' or 'Father' or 'Here am I and here are You' makes a world of difference. Just as lying in the sun doing nothing, surrendering your body to it, with the sun blazing down on you, affects your body and your senses, so this surrendering of the soul to that transforming Power affects the soul, and I believe that as truly as the sun changes the colour of your skin so that Power changes you at the centre.

To see God was to be delivered from all fear and weakness. 'Remember this', she writes in a letter, '—grip it and get it working spontaneously—God is the biggest force in any circumstances.' And again: 'I would say that circumstances are *for* you when you've *really* got contact with God and some of His strength, and that comes by believing in that contact in every tiny minute, looking up and saying: "I'm so glad You're here all the time." '

Have faith in God. Faith is really believing that a *good* will come
to pass in spite of things that are looking clean contrary. Dis-
belief, indifference, boredom, fear, they will come at you like
swarms of gnats. Watch them, from outside yourself. Go on
believing in the truth. Whether the thing that baffles you (that
personal relationship) looks possible or impossible is really not
your question. You have your task in it, but you will be beaten
in it if you let go faith in the fact that God also has His task in it.
He will bring about the issue, not you.

To keep looking at God and not at oneself and one's sins was
for her the secret of spiritual growth.

Isn't 'He brought me forth into a large place; He delivered me
because He delighted in me' delightful? It's a higher conception
of God than the 'miserable sinner' conception—more effective
every way. If you kept your face on the Father, you would
gradually trample on your sins. You would keep climbing up,
and you would climb much more quickly than if you stayed
groping on, and looking at your sins. Real sins, for a weak
nature, are such consuming things. We can't do anything
unless we have a spiritual passion greater than the sinful passion,
and it will have to be enormous.

'Florence', writes one of her friends, 'not only declared God to
be big beyond our conceiving, but her actions agreed with her
words. She never limited the love, the generosity and understanding of God, and consequently there was no limit to her
own love, generosity and understanding.' 'You could go to her
room,' says another, 'and at first be intensely aware of her, but
after talking with her you would leave the room almost oblivious
of her because you were so much more aware of God.'

To Florence's seeing the fundamental evil was that God to-day
has been pushed into the background and is no longer the central
fact of life. 'The struggle of life for us who call ourselves Christians
is the struggle to get God into the first place in our lives.' The
subordination of God was the essence of the worldly spirit.
When she made her visit to East Africa towards the close of her
life that was the concern which forced itself on her attention.
'You're all so *good*,' she would exclaim. 'Everywhere I go, everyone is up so early, so busy, so good. Yet everywhere God is so

much in the background. We are more important than God, the Government is more important than God, the educational inspector is more important than God, our moods are more important than God.'

To recover a sense of the ever-present, all-important reality of God seemed to Florence the most urgent task of our time.

Some of us [she quotes in one of her addresses] will have to enter upon a vow of dedication to the eternal which is as complete and irrevocable as was the vow of the monks in the middle ages. Little groups of utterly dedicated lives knowing each other in fellowship with the Divine; to live in the world, but not wholly of the world. Religion has become dulled and cooled and flooded with the secular; it must be lit and fired and flooded with the eternal. They must be ready to go the second half, obedient, sensitive, selfless. Such groups could revive the Christian witness and shake the countryside.

God meant everything to Florence, because it meant that love was the supreme and ultimate thing in the universe. When Christianity had failed, it 'was always because the overwhelming pressure of spiritual mediocrity diluted the Christian obedience to the stark demand of God's bed-rock quality of love'. Love was for Florence 'the greatest adventure of all in the Christian life'. 'You see', she writes in a letter, 'I really am keener on love than anything else in the world.'

Love for her meant a high and costly achievement. 'Love', she writes, 'is the only way. It would be easier to practise, if it were only love. It's because it's love *and* truth that it's so difficult.' And in another letter in characteristic fashion, speaking of some one she had met, she writes, 'She is full of pose, but she has no end of guts. I begin to think that guts come next to love; anyway, love without them is a flimsy, sentimental thing.'

Love and humility seemed to Florence the only values that counted in the eternal world. She knew that it was the contemplation of God's love that alone could kindle and keep burning a flame of love. That flame was kindled in Florence by the contemplation of Christ. In her pursuit of perfection what she had before her was no abstract ideal of sanctity, but the living image of Christ.

I have been thinking why being a missionary is like being an actress. Isn't it because you long to get the *feel* of Jesus Christ inside you—to *feel* what He *felt* when some one hurt or disappointed Him? An actress does the same—tries to get what the character felt. I think perhaps that's it. You are wanting to be that other, and for us that other is Christ. I want to feel gay like He felt when people are trying to get one down. He is feeling, 'I am with my Father'—not with the little devils in your spirit that make you unhappy.

'Above everything else', writes one of her close friends, 'Jesus Christ was a living reality to her.' She was fond of quoting Maeterlinck's saying that 'the soul can never be happy if it possess not, and love not, something that is pure', and she would dilate on the immense joy of loving something that is pure. She was captured by Christ's perfection of living. She had fallen in love with His way of doing things. She always spoke of Him as some one intensely real to her. She talked of Him in the most natural way, and those who listened to her were conscious that what she was saying was something that she knew in her own experience. 'When you love a person very much', she used to say, 'you never forget it; it's a glow at the back of everything. We all ought to love Jesus like that.'

In a follower of Jesus Christ, she always insisted, His whole work of redemption must be re-enacted in the arena of life. His incarnation, death and resurrection are experiences through which the individual must again and again pass. 'I wish for you', she says in a letter, 'suffering and agonies and the supreme and enduring joy of achievement. Anything else is fatuous, if you've seen Jesus at all.'

She was continually discovering fresh aspects of Him. What you have helped me to see [she writes to a friend] is a very happy Christ. I can't get away from that. He's not saying, 'Be like this and you'll be good'. He's saying, 'Be like this and you'll be happy, and it's the only way of happiness'. It's not how other people affect you, it's how you affect other people that matters all the time. Give and give and give happiness, and you'll get it all the time. That's the way God has made things work, and this stupid me, wanting to get away from the pain of this place, sees now and then that *that* wouldn't make me happy. It's accepting it that makes me happy, and I have been very happy lately, since I have seen the happy Christ.

Her love for Christ was an anchor which held fast in all perplexities. In her last visit to East Africa she was urging a group of missionaries to study astronomy and learn about the wonders of the universe, because 'our conception of God is too small.' One of those present said that all this immensity frightened her and shook her faith. Florence's face was immediately lit up with a smile and she replied, 'But you must learn to look at it and say, "I believe in Jesus". You have to look straight at *everything* and say, "I believe in Jesus".'

It was the contemplation of Jesus that would make possible the quality of love which He demanded.

If I have any advice to give at all, I would beg you to study Jesus Christ in His dealings with men, until the stand He takes every time glows and burns within your hearts, so that you yourselves can do no other when the same things happen to you, and I would beg you to pray that you may learn to love as Jesus Christ loved, with more passion and with more insistency than anything you have ever prayed for in your life, and then refuse defeat. Perhaps you will be able to do no more, but refuse defeat!

The difference which Florence believed this *seeing* of Jesus would make in practice is shown by two illustrations.

It's *always* been the religious people [she writes in a letter] who do the awful things. Don't you see it's because they haven't *seen*. To see things squarely, being a missionary, an archdeacon or a headmistress in Africa is often a better job than anything the same type of person could get in England. They're Somebody, with a large S. They like it. It's that they aren't really Christ's, they're religious perhaps, but they're not Christ's. They haven't *seen*, do you see? They need infinitely more to be saved than the raw heathen.

Again in a letter to a former student working in Africa she writes:

K

You see if Jesus had met A—— with that leering look of his, His heart would have been full of pity that this child was possessed of a devil for the time being, and He would have healed him and A—— would have fallen at His feet—healed. We are so powerless to be that releasing channel because 'self' feelings block up the way. We do not *see* God because we blind ourselves, get side tracked by seeing the man as horrible. That wrong seeing blinds the rest of our seeing, but one day you will stand before A—— with *nothing* but a vast pity in your heart and then, though you may not see it, something will happen to A——. I believe that, and for everyone you touch when you get there.

Florence knew in her own experience the effects which such a divinely inspired pity might have. Her colleague in Uganda was in one of her furious tempers. She had hurled at Florence bitter and hurtful words. Florence remained silent. 'O God', she prayed inwardly, 'help me to be *sorry*—to love her.' She clung desperately to the thought of God's infinite pity. Suddenly the angry words ceased, and the older woman said, 'You will never know what you have done for me,' and went quietly to her own room.

Because love was for Florence the joy and prize of life, she was utterly impatient with the preoccupation with self, in herself or in others, that blocked the way to this fulfilment. No note recurs so frequently in her letters as the intensity of her desire for liberation from self. She wanted nothing more than to '*cut out* this self-importance, this egotism, which keeps us small and foot-bound, and holds us back from giving our true selves their freedom'. She knew well that 'the dissipation of egoism is always a terrible, tearing, tormenting process, but without it there is no hope of grasping something beyond.'

Because it barred the way to growth, pre-occupation with self seemed to her unaccountably 'silly'. 'It isn't worth *dallying* with idiotic pride and sour tempers, it just isn't worth while.' 'It's so *silly* to let a person who is tied in prison and kicking make us personal about the kicks.' 'Getting rid of the self is only the means of freeing you to love. It's so simple I can't think why you all *like* to grip on, like grim death, to any self-defence at all. You may say and *feel* that you want to run; *you*, the intrinsic you, doesn't. It wants to stay safe inside its own little temperamental walls.'

But to indulge the self was not only folly but disloyalty. 'Wherever we are there are small situations going wrong, and we are to redeem them, but if we start on the way of redemption and refuse when it begins to make us suffer, whether it is our pride, or our nerves, or our comfort, we are most horribly disloyal.' 'The world is rotting with self. Oh why is it? Why won't people see?'

Above all, freedom from self was the necessary condition of being able to help others. Only those who had escaped from self to something bigger could lead others out of the wasteland.

Many Christians [she says in a paper on 'Leadership'] have been shown the first mile of the Christian venture, salvation from sin, but not the second, salvation from egotism, and that is where they begin to wander in a wasteland. We too have to know this thing deep in our bones, salvation from the egotism that puts the self before God. It is a long and costly business to learn. Unless we are always learning ourselves— a learning that will free us from any tinge of complacency that we are safe because we know such a lot of theory, or are able to run effectively some Christian enterprise or institution —we can lead no one out of their wasteland. So many refuse to face themselves in any deep and costing way, and that is why there are comparatively few spiritual leaders.

I don't know [she wrote in a letter] whether I feel anything extra big coming. I believe that, if our eyes were open, we would be seeing that it is here. The Spirit *is* here, swaying through individuals and groups and, if only we will obey, it will go through the larger groups, nations and races. But, we won't clear the rubbish from our own spirits.

Florence knew that in answer to her earnest seeking deliverance from self had in large measure been granted to her. 'I don't quite know how I lost this self-importance and occupation with self. I never spend a minute hardly thinking about myself. I just left myself and loved God and other people.' 'I don't matter to myself any more', she was able to say towards the close of her life.

Here, again, we come upon paradox—the great paradox of the

Christian life. Florence's constant emphasis was on self-naughting; her primary concern was to get completely rid of self. At the same time she could declare with the whole force of her being, 'Isn't it lovely to be alive?' We have seen how she rejoiced in the beauty of God's creation. Having renounced the world in any self-seeking sense, she had experienced the truth of the saying, 'All things are yours'. Having lost her life, she had found it. Having been reborn into a new dimension of life in the unrestricted love of God and her fellow human beings, her delight in the world that God had made became for her a continual act of worship. The enjoyment of beauty meant for her an entrance into more abundant life.

She passionately believed that all beauty has its source in God, and for this reason constantly strove to make beautiful the place in which God's children live. To do this was to beautify her Father's house, to glorify Him, to reveal Him to others. Whenever her means allowed she would spend lavishly on some object of beauty or art, denying herself in some other respect in order to be able to do it. In all this she found an exemplar in the woman who brought an alabaster jar of ointment, very costly, and poured it on Jesus' head—a story which she greatly loved.

In Florence's attitude to beauty there is a remarkable originality and freshness. She broke with what has been the prevailing tradition of Christian community life. She took no vow of poverty. One would have to travel far to find a community house that could compare with St Julian's in the beauty of its equipment and its surroundings. Complete dedication to God meant for Florence an attempt to bring the realm of beauty into subjection to Christ. When St Anthony left the security of his village to live in the tombs, part of his purpose was to conquer the desert, with its fearsome and untamed forces for Christ, in order to prove that the old gods were demons who vanished with the dawn. St Francis' desire in espousing poverty was in part to prove that the life of a tramp or casual labourer could be dedicated as completely to the Lord as the life of the cloister with its recognized status and rights. Florence followed neither of these courses. She did not choose total insecurity nor did she live in the wilderness. But she did, in her own words, 'go the whole hog', and that is the essence of the dedicated life. Poverty of spirit, the denial of self, she sought with her whole heart. And in the measure that she found it, she found herself at the same time at home in her Father's world to worship Him in the totality of His creation.

Her own view of the matter finds expression, not in a considered statement but in one of her letters, in which she so often reveals, as it were casually, her deeper thoughts. The letter was written while she was engaged in missionary training.

About possessions, it seems to me it's like everything else perhaps. You have to go the whole hog if you want to do anything really worth while. And you can't go the whole hog about more than one thing at a time in life. I don't think you can go the whole hog about a thing unless you know you *can't* do otherwise. Then it becomes vocation. You can't take the ideal of poverty if you live in our conditions, at least I can't in this job at the moment, because the one thing people are failing in is in any idea of beauty. The attempt to be economical has meant that the whole of the training has degenerated into shoddiness, not only in material things, but it has all seeped through to the finer issues too. I have had to push everything on to something better, because the whole thing seemed to be founded on 'it will do'. Money is nothing ultimately, when it comes to spiritual values. A vocation to poverty is quite a different thing from being economical.

The whole thing, I believe, is to be positive about what you are going to do. And I've been positive about trying to build something that is more dignified. I think there is a vocation for riches just as much as there is for poverty, to balance up the people who are *content* to be shoddy. I don't mind as long as a bilious green carpet gives me a pain every time I look at it, but when I get used to it then I fight to get a new one. I don't really want to accumulate possessions, but I do want beautiful surroundings and dignified things. Clothes with a good cut to them because if you get something dignified in the way of material things it gives you a stable bit of rock in your mind. My background has always been so unstable that perhaps I put too much stress on that.

And at the end she adds, as she often does when she has been saying something very penetrating, 'I believe I'm talking the most awful rot'.

While in her attempt to found a Christian Community Florence diverged from one emphasis in the Christian tradition her outlook had the closest affinity with another. The consecration of beauty to the worship of God found prodigal expression in the building of the cathedrals in the early middle ages. 'This art', it has been said, 'because it grew directly from a deep religious purpose and feeling, was shared by the multitude. Tens of thousands of people were employed on it, and all gave to it something of their inner selves, something that welled up unconsciously from their deepest instincts.'[1] The same God-given human delight in design is seen in the endless care lavished on illuminated manuscripts of the Gospels and Psalter.

Florence's devotion to beauty had its roots in the sense that, if you love God with your whole heart, you must for His sake do your very best in all that you do. If you run a college, everything in it must teach. If you are in charge of a mission-station you must make the whole ensemble, the buildings and the grounds, eloquent of the grace which you proclaim. If you provide a guest house you must make it as beautiful and refreshing as lies in your power.

Florence knew also that the wider a man's natural and human interests, the richer is the material which grace can transfigure and the Holy Spirit can use. She had sat at the feet of Baron von Hügel and had learned from him that

the soul cannot attain to its fullest possible spiritual development without the vigorous specific action and differentiation of forces and functions of a not directly religious character, which will have to energize, each according to its own intrinsic nature, within the ever ampler, and ever more closely-knit, organization of the complete life of the soul.[2]

There is, of course, no simple or final reconciliation of the conflicting claims that life makes on the individual. The insistent voice of the unhappy, the disturbing appeal of 'some life of men unblest,' is constantly at strife with the individual delight in beauty and its creation. There is no escape from the competition

[1] Barton, *Purpose and Admiration,* p. 51.
[2] *The Mystical Element of Religion,* Vol. II, p. 393.

and tension in any single, once-for-all decision but only in daily renewed acts of obedience to the call of God in the living present.

In Florence the love of beauty and creation had its ordered place in a life wholly surrendered to the controlling love of God and man. Her devotion to beauty was far more for the sake of others than for herself. At Barns Green she had a room outside the main building, and later lived in a converted loft over a garage, and she insisted, when there was a choice, on having in her own room the older and shabbier furniture; the beautiful things were for the guests. It was said at the beginning of the chapter that her life was conspicuous for the balance and symmetry of its proportions. The love of God, the love of man, the love of God's creation— to this order she consistently adhered and, at the cost of un-questioning obedience and daily self-discipline, she worked out a pattern of life of such richness that it will for long continue to unfold fresh meanings.

It must not be supposed that the insights and conquests that have been described in this chapter were easily won. Florence kept no account of the doubts that assailed her inner life. Her thoughts were too fully engaged with God and other people for her to keep a record of her own struggles. She began a private journal about the year 1941, but the entries in it are few and far between, and no other record of a similar nature exists among her papers. There is, however, one entry near the beginning which shows that she was not free from deep questionings. It reads:

Of course, there is God. If only He would *once* become visible. Whatever they say, it isn't easy to love someone you never see or hear. How queer it is. I have set a course towards Him and the two commandments. I have talked a lot about them and in a kind of watered down and fitful way followed them. It's these two commandments, though, that haunt me to-night. To set my purpose tighter round them? I wonder.

The problem of suffering haunted Florence all through her life. She says in a letter written in the year she spent at Storrington:

I have never read or heard anyone say anything yet that *quite* touched the vastness and depth of suffering. I think it's because I can't quite understand God 'sharing' what it *seemed*

He might have helped—earthquakes, tidal waves, and the horrors of such things. I know they can't be explained and you have got to trust beyond them, but that's my struggle, my particular one.

And in another letter:

I had a dreadful affair last week with a baby rabbit caught in a trap, caught most horribly, and we had to kill it and couldn't find a large enough stone. Every detail was too awful. I don't want to tell you. It upset me for days. I simply couldn't pray. I felt I hated being forced into such an awful affair. Why did God leave me to kill it? It wasn't until I began gambling on 'God is love' again that it became at all bearable, and then on Sunday we went to Communion and it suddenly sprang out at me that God was giving me the cup—not as He generally gives it, in Communion, but quite definitely asking me to have the patience to drink those kind of tiny sips of His Cup. Am I rambling? It sounds queer, doesn't it?

The difficulties of the *practice* of the Christian life are more often mentioned. 'I know it's difficult', 'It isn't easy' are phrases that occur frequently in letters. 'I find life gets so much happier', she writes in one letter, 'with a kind of steady inner happiness that I long for people to find it, and you can find it only by going the way you were created to go. Why it was made quite so difficult I can't think. Perhaps we shall never know in this bit of earth life, but there it is.' She knew 'on her pulses' the immense difficulties of the Christian life. Those who lived with her remember how often she would say: 'The first thing I shall ask God when I am free of the body is why He makes it all so difficult.'

The Christian life was difficult because Christianity for Florence was not something that you professed, or talked about, or thought you believed, but something which you *lived*. That is why she sought unceasingly to become more 'real'. 'I want terribly to see truth about myself, so that I can be real; unreality stops all growth.' 'You will never know what real struggling does in this place. But I know a bit, and I have learnt in more than any other way how any *reality* affects other lives and your surroundings. Something living goes out of you.' 'Those who possess truth', she was fond of quoting, 'because they have lived it, are *sought* by others; whereas those who are chiefly concerned with the propagation of doctrine have to seek an audience.' The St Julian's Community, she believed, could help other people only if its members had in an *exceptional degree* overcome evil. In her own life word and deed had in remarkable measure become one.

She was by nature a fighter. 'You often wonder', she wrote, 'how far you ought to lie down and take things and how far you ought to get up and fight. To fight is in my bones; what I need is to be made gentle.' She never avoided difficulties nor tried to find a way round them. Wherever she saw evil entrenched her impulse was always to go out and attack it.

Florence was conscious, especially in her later years, of a certain loneliness. Her pursuit was so eager that she left others in the rear and went on alone. Every letter from those closest to her contains the phrase, or some equivalent of it, 'we were all so far behind'. She wrote herself:

> Sometimes I feel quite baffled. So many people love only the mediocre, and they love in me my mediocrity which has a bit more power in it than in theirs. But they don't love my struggle for the pure and perfect. That clashes. That is where I begin to be tiresome to them. It does nothing but elude their want. They will see *me*. They will not try to see what I want to make them see because it is better than this thing that is me.

Her desire for perfection was in part a natural gift. 'Some of the young missionaries were saying', she once wrote, 'that it was so hopeless to work under some of the younger men. But, if I were told to do something I knew was second-best, I couldn't do it, could you? I'd rather be turned out. Can you imagine a group of people sitting down while they see a youngish man making hay of the education? I can't understand it.' It was, of course, particular individuals she had in mind, not younger men missionaries as a class.

But this natural disposition to covet what is excellent was enormously deepened by her contemplation of Christ's perfection.

> Jesus demanded the impossible. Why should He die for you to help you to do something you could do for yourself? Let

L

us be quite sure of that. He watered down nothing. Good deeds were not enough. Even love was not enough unless it was love of a certain kind—the kind that wrung from St Paul that dreadful cry, 'Though I give all my goods to feed the poor, though I give my body to be burned and have not love, it profiteth me nothing'.

If the life that is in us is to be the life that inspires and educates, it must be a life lived always on the high levels of *love, joy, peace*. These are the fruits of the Spirit and to bring them into every detail of life is the hardest task any one could be asked to do.

She was impressed with a saying of Péguy: 'A word is not the same with one writer as with another. One tears it from the guts, the other pulls it out of his overcoat pocket.' She comments on it in a letter. 'I do see that so plainly—it's because some people won't go down as far as the guts, only as far as pockets, so how can they use words from anywhere else? But why live life from a pocket? It is so wasteful.'

But few could really run with her at these levels. Her spirit scaled heights that others could not reach. The sense of loneliness was often with her and she knew both its benediction and its cost. She had often to turn back and wait for others when she wanted to press ahead. This was trying for a disposition naturally quick and impatient. She was apt to be impatient in argument and discussion. She would often brook no contradictions. Yet she was able to conquer and control her impatience and what impressed others was often the supernatural quality of her patience and understanding.

She was, I suppose, impatient [writes one of her friends]. It was part of her, as much as the swiftness with which she moved, and the sensitiveness which caught any falsity or any unhappiness in her surroundings before anyone else knew of it. She wanted to move on, all the time, further into a world which she knew to be God's world; and those who sensed this—and I can only call it a 'divine impatience'—know also how unhesitatingly she would wait for those who were trying to follow, but at how much slower a pace. The thing we cannot know, any of us, is what the cost to her of such a discipline must have been.

Florence would be the first to pour scorn on any attempt to represent her as perfect. But it is the simple truth that her self-conquest was so real, her pre-occupation with God and the other person so constant, that it was only on rare occasions that her friends were able to observe any flaw in her selflessness or any failure to live the truth as she saw it. When she was at fault or made a mistake she at once made an apology. If there was momentary impatience, it was quickly brought under control. The verdict of a keen observer, who lived with her for the last ten years and, apart from occasional absences, saw her every day, is 'I have loved some one who seemed perfect, and yet was so human.'

If, when she was about to start the St Julian's experiment, Florence seemed to question her basic principles, the temptation was a passing one. Never did her certainty about the two great commandments being the clue to the meaning of life shine more brightly and unintermittently than during the last decade of her life. Whatever inward struggles she may have had in her striving for perfection, she kept largely to herself. To the outward world she turned a smiling and undaunted face. To others she appeared a rock of strength. None of those who knew her will deny that the characteristic notes of her life were those of confidence, conquest and joy.

When I first met her [writes one of her old students], she impressed me—startled me—with a quality I can best call life, that vivid flame-like quality, so much more than mere moral goodness, which crackles through all the greatest saints. Florence used often to wonder why there are so few *alive* people in the world—'such a lot of nice, pleasant people, such crowds of conquered people, and so few conquering'.

'*No* situation is impossible', she writes. 'If you believe that it is, you have no message of salvation.' 'I am getting obsessed about this weak giving in to failure. We needn't.' Refusal to be defeated was for Florence the *pivot* on which spiritual growth depends. 'Refuse to accept defeat' was the advice she gave over and over again in her letters.

And what in the world [she says in one of her talks], when you come to think of it, has all that beaten down beauty to do with people who have glad tidings for mankind? Only a spirit freeing itself till it is free can have glad tidings to tell to anyone else. The sight of conquered Christians is the real desperate tragedy of this day. When you think of the early Church, it had no buildings, no fixed organisation, no New Testament, no vocabulary of its own. It just had a body of men who were pressing towards a mark of a calling that wasn't coming from earth at all. It was coming from Heaven. A store of teaching of how to work out the progress of the Spirit, and gladness that there was a divinely given power militant, conquering, changing, transforming, not once but all the time, their minds, hearts and whole life, bringing them all one by one into the bright safety of the beauty of Love.

The Christian life was for Florence not painful conformity to a code but a splendid adventure in search of truth and beauty.

I don't think you will get out [she writes to a friend] by being gooder, but by flinging something to the winds. Don't pray to be made gooder, but to be made looser and lighter. It's the poets and lovers who get there.

If we could remember, not the tiresome endless dying but that it is a true and inevitable law that *some beauty is born every time. Believe that*—what fun to die, one more bud on our tree of life and love and beauty. That faith would do it, you know. I see myself as two—one shadowy, dark figure, rather shirking along, always clutching at what is small, low and mean and depressing; and the other, free and erect, and shaking its hair back in the sun. I'm trying to see myself like that, and to refuse to own the one, and quickly to take the other; but a good swipe at the dark one, even giggle when I've swiped it.

If we look at the ranks of people over forty, there is as a rule no passionate quality of spiritual force, ardent and growing. On the other side are those sensitive spirits in whom we can see a great spreading of consciousness, awareness, a clear intensity of vision, a steady control over circumstances. The mind is not screwed down so tightly to the work-a-day world but has become attuned to a deeper rhythm. They have the victory of a forward moving spirit. They have found that which is at the heart of every prophet's vision, which every artist struggles to communicate, and which all great music tries to utter—the rich yet simple revelation of God.

Whatever the devilish thing is that keeps us all from this intended spirit's beauty—its horror is in its insidious subtle power to keep you just on the verge. Always on the verge of something truer.

Perhaps I am looking for too much; but religion to me really is *a song*, not this everlasting absorption in sin. That stops the singing, *so must go*, and there is trouble and stupidity in our sin, but we need not contaminate with it the song that religion is; we can keep that clear.

In the last address she gave, when her last illness had already begun, she gave expression to her central faith.

It is a hard way, but everyone who has known this 'losing your life to find it' tells us how, as the mind and desire go the way of self-naughting more simply and readily with practice, you do know that you are living in a new and fresh world; that at the root of you, instead of the old unease, the old feeling of guilt, the lovelessness, there is a content, happy shining, whatever comes, a great and smiling content.

If God is love, and we were made to love as the stars were made to shine, then every creature is desirous of finding this disinterested love. This love is not meant to die. It is the fire and energy of the Spirit. We wonder why we grow discouraged and flat, why there is so little spiritual force in us, why life seems dry. If only we could get away from self into something outside ourselves, greater than ourselves, then our spirits would kindle love and burn with ever renewing life. We should discover that we were alive and happy in a new way, because we had found our true nature and were poised from a steady centre. We should have found eternal life, God's own way to love.

Professor C. H. Dodd, in one of his recent broadcast talks, describes in these words the picture of Jesus of Nazareth presented in St Mark's Gospel: 'His vivid and forceful speech, His poet's insight into nature and the human soul, His ready sympathy—but also on occasion His devastating severity—His integrity and strength of purpose, His power to command, and His tremendous energy.' Better words could hardly be found to sum up the account that has been given of one who desired above everything to be conformed to His image.

XV

LAST DAYS

THE MOVE to the new house at Coolham had been made in January, 1950. The house looked out on a lovely sheet of water and beyond was the satisfying line of the downs crowned by Chanctonbury. The gardens had been well kept but none of the newcomers knew what they contained, and that first unforgettable Spring was full of fresh surprises. A member of the Community writes:

> It began on the morning when Florence found a huge clump of snowdrops at the water's edge; the sun was shining so brightly that you could not see the whiteness till it was at your feet and then it burst on you, a revelation of purity. From that day the garden was a succession of unfolding beauty as the spring went its way. In the little woodland path to the lake, first there were clumps of gold and purple crocuses which gave way to the blue of scillas and clumps of primroses and later violet windflowers and banks of daffodils and narcissi, which in their turn gave way to pools of bluebells. In the shrubbery and orchard and round the lake were all the trees in bridal array—flowering sprays of cherry, peach, apple, hawthorn, so that you met clouds of pink and white wherever you looked. It was a long dream of loveliness. During those spring days Florence often said, 'If earth can be like this, it makes me gasp to think what heaven could be like.' Looking back, it seems as though in the beauty of that spring there was a hint and a promise to her of eternal life holding out its arms to her.

On May 19th Florence complained of having been kept awake by an irritating rash. It was the beginning of her last illness. She was due to go to Worcester on May 23rd to give an address and to pay a visit. As she was very unwell, the journey was made by car. She thought on the way that she would not be equal to the address, but she went through with it. Quotations from this last address have been made in earlier pages. On the last evening of her visit she went with her friends to Stratford and saw *Measure for Measure*, which she greatly enjoyed. On the way home she was evidently really ill. When she reached St Julian's she was put to bed, and the rash became worse.

The doctor diagnosed the trouble as nettle-rash, and there was no thought of her being dangerously ill. But the rash became steadily worse, and the doctor decided to try to get a bed in St Thomas's Home attached to St Thomas's hospital, where an attempt could be made to get to the root of the trouble, and she was taken there in the second week of June. For the first few days friends were able to visit her. Then all visitors were forbidden on the ground that she needed to be kept under drugs and it was not good for her to rouse herself in order to talk. The specialist was able at last to diagnose the trouble as Hodgkin's disease. Visitors were again permitted to see her, and two friends were able to be with her day and night at the end. Throughout her illness she was gentle, trustful and childlike. She was wont to say that character was revealed in illness. As in health, so in sickness her thought was always not of herself, but of those around her. She was unconscious for the last few days. She passed away at ten o'clock on Monday, July 3rd.

The service at the cremation was conducted by the Bishop of St Albans, Dr Michael Gresford Jones, the son of her life-long friends. In the following week, on July 12th, a memorial service was held at St Botolph's, Bishopsgate, at which the Bishop of Worcester gave the address.

Following the cremation, the ashes were scattered very early in the morning on the downs which she dearly loved, above Storrington.

The road from Storrington to the downs, [writes one who took part] rose into early morning mist as we went up, and the air was full of the scent of lime blossom and wild thyme. We stood at the top gazing at the distances over which Florence had loved to look. On one side, the sea, on the other side, the woods and farms, the patterned countryside. It was like being on the roof of the world, and the silence and the mist closed round us. But by a sort of natural miracle, in the few moments that it took to scatter her ashes there, the cloud thinned, and the pale, washed-blue sky was overhead, and the country down below was suddenly there in sunlight, cornfields and farms, hedges and roads, and the lifting sweep of downland across to the sea. And when the wind took hold of the ashes so that they were a little, light cloud, the whole sky seemed to be full of skylarks, in a burst of song, and the air was filled with their singing. We stood in the middle of it and knew that no prayer was necessary for all prayers were said.

My clearest picture of Florence [writes one of her friends] will always be of her in the new St Julian's in the early mornings before breakfast, feeding the swans at the edge of the lake. This was a morning ritual and I always felt my day was incomplete when I didn't see her, tall and swiftly moving over the bars of light on the lawn, over the sharp shadows and the patches of sun, dressed in her gay overall, to where the two great swans waited at the water's edge. There they would rear up their wings and their arched necks and she would give them the scraps of bread. Swans are alarming creatures when they are big ones, and when they are close to one: they look immensely powerful and they have a habit of advancing with ferocious hiss and raised wing feathers, so that I for one would never stand my ground. Florence was always straight and unyielding, and she was the only person I ever saw who never took one step backwards, or seemed uncertain. I used to watch this morning ritual day after day, and week after week, and it gives me a picture of her that always has the bright edges of summer and early morning about it. The day after Florence died we were back again at St Julian's—the swans left the lake. They went quite suddenly, unnoticed between one day and the next. There is another lake not many miles distant, and they presumably went to that. But it gave one a curious plunge to the heart somehow. They were so much part of our picture of Florence and of her joy in creation.

Florence had once quoted in a letter to a friend the lines of a poem by Edna St Vincent Millay—

I looked in my heart while the wild swans went over,
And what did I see I had not seen before?
Only a question less or a question more;
Nothing to match the flight of wild birds flying.

She went on, 'Think of that when you get clogged up with petty talk—"nothing to match the flight of wild birds flying." There's a lovely little sentence I always remember and use as a prayer —"God keep me something of the world untamed." These sordid dusty ways of ours do so *tame* the beauty in us.'

She had never looked on death, whether her own or that of her friends, as a tragedy but as a joyous, exciting adventure. This earthly life for her was just a 'first brief rush into existence,' with all the eternal years ahead to grow into the full life of God. A friend recalls that, on the last occasion on which she saw her, when they sat looking out on a summer evening on one of the transparent days in May, she asked Florence whether she ever knew those 'apprehensions of the dark' which trouble most of us at one time or another, and was given this reply:

I can never see why one should fear to die. When I walk into the garden here early in the morning and nearly burst with excitement at this world; and when I realize that it is only a shadow, a pale ghost of what *that* world must be like—then I can only feel a tremendous longing to know more of it, and to be in it.

XVI

PROSPECT

FLORENCE ALLSHORN was always moving on. If she had lived, she might have come to feel about St Julian's, as she did about missionary training, that she had set a course which others could follow further, and that she was being called to some fresh creative task. That was not given her on earth. If she could speak to us now, she would say what she used often to say while she was here: 'Christianity is to-day, and to-morrow, the past is only material.' The continuance of her work and the task of fresh creation is left to those of us who are still alive.

The members of the Community will carry on the work of St Julian's, including the farm and the children's house. This will involve for them a deeper apprehension of the purpose which inspired her, and for the time being an effort of consolidation rather than of expansion. The experience of the past ten years is against making too definite plans for the future, and forcing developments to conform to them. It points rather to the need for maintaining an attitude of expectancy, of remaining eager and alert for any new call, and of responding to demands as they come.

But the life of Florence Allshorn has a significance too rich and wide to be exhausted in the continuance of her work at St Julian's. Nor can it be measured only by the fact that many who never knew her may through the record of her life catch the contagion of her faith, her joy in life, her surrender to the power of love and her indomitable purpose. What makes her life important is not so much her personal achievement as the relevance of her vision of life to the needs of our time. She herself would have vehemently asserted that her individual life was neither here nor there and that the only thing that mattered was what she was *seeing*. With the clarity that is given only to those who are willing to live their vision she saw the truths on which the recovery of mankind depends. The two great commandments were the master lights of *all* her seeing. Love as the ultimate truth and meaning of human existence, love as a splendid and supremely satisfying good to be realized in action, love as liberty, victory and joy—these are the great realities of which her life was the embodiment.

The call did not come to her, as it did to many Christian saints in the past, to espouse poverty, though she envisaged that as a possible vocation and would have joyfully followed it, if it had been demanded of her. She did not spend her life in the service of the outcasts of society, though they at once became her friends when they crossed her path. It was not her mission to minister to the physical necessities of the destitute, the broken and the diseased, though she immediately responded to such needs when she encountered them. Her distinctive vocation was to show that the ordinary relations of daily life offer a field for the heroic practice of Christian love. In the range and depth of her understanding of what this means and in her relentless pursuit of conformity to Christ's standards she was to a large extent a path-finder. The changes that are taking place in modern society are likely to give an increasing importance to the trail that she blazed. In proportion as society as a whole assumes responsibility for the physical care and primary needs of all its members, the opportunities of conspicuous voluntary service by individuals in relieving the physical necessities of their fellows must inevitably contract. But in no form of society will there cease to be need for the manifestations of love with which Florence Allshorn was primarily concerned. The relations of persons with persons are, and will always continue to be, the stuff and substance of a truly human life.

It is very easy to misunderstand and to *trivialize* any emphasis on the importance of the relations between persons. Florence's sense of proportion was too strong to allow her to isolate the relation of two particular individuals from its larger context and to treat it as an end in itself. That was something she could dismiss as 'these niggardly little troubles of relationships'. It was the fact that failure to overcome these troubles should block the way to more important things that gave her concern. Her real intention can best be understood by remembering that the subject was forced on her attention by her experience as a missionary. What seemed to her to be at stake was the fruitfulness of the whole missionary enterprise and the supreme values for which it stood.

The expansion of the Christian Church throughout the world was one of the important events of the nineteenth century.

In the recent past, through its missionary enterprises [writes Professor John Macmurray in his recent book], it has established itself in all the great centres of the world's population, and everywhere exerts an influence far in excess of its numerical strength. When we add to this the indirect effects of its civilizing influence through the centuries, we are bound to conclude not merely that it is a significant factor in the problem that faces civilization, but that there is no other factor which can rival it in importance. In a very real and practical sense it is the only instrument for the achievement of a community of the world which we possess.[1]

This judgment will seem to many an exaggeration. If there were a more general acceptance of Professor Macmurray's scale of values, it might meet with a wider agreement.

But just as in society as a whole the advances of science and technics have created what has been called a 'second nature' of mechanization and organization, which is in some ways more frightening, more uncontrollable and more difficult to change than original nature, so the expansion of the missionary movement and the necessity of co-operating with governments in such matters as health and education have brought about a degree of organization in which everything tends to be subordinated to keeping the machine running and to the efficient performance of the job. This was the immense danger that Florence Allshorn perceived and set herself to combat. If the Church succumbed to the dominance of organization, and set the 'job' before right human relations, it would cease to be the manifestation of love and an example of community. It would fail in the purpose for

[1] *Conditions of Freedom* (Faber and Faber, 1950), p. 98.

which it has been set in the world. The salt would lose its savour, and the chief hope of the world would fade. For the maintenance and increase of human fellowship is, as Professor Macmurray says, 'the function of religion, and the achievement of an inclusive human fellowship is a religious task.' No one of her generation perceived the crucial nature of this issue more clearly than Florence Allshorn and no one made a more determined effort to do something practical about it. She set herself to create the conditions out of which something new and vitalizing might grow.

It was the sense that the faithfulness of the Church to its divine commission was at stake that drove Florence to take the line that she did. But what she set herself to do was at the same time a service to the good of society as a whole. Our present technical and industrial society, which is extending its influence throughout the whole world, has for a long time, as Professor V. A. Demant is constantly reminding us, been living on human capital—that is, on the habits and virtues bred and fostered by a pre-industrial society. There has over large areas of life been a progressive decay of human *substance*, that is, of the qualities and attitudes that belong to a genuinely human existence. The renewal of society, consequently, cannot be brought about by large-scale measures devised and put into operation by those at the top. It is only as individuals and small groups acquire a new outlook and attitude, and as these spread silently and imperceptibly from one to another in ever widening circles that forces are set in motion that can bring about a real renewal. The late Professor Karl Mannheim, a friend of Florence Allshorn and a great admirer of St Julian's, in his posthumous work *Freedom, Power and Democratic Planning*, recognizes that institutional reforms by themselves are inadequate 'without a remaking of man and reconditioning of human behaviour,' and devotes the final section of his book (nearly half of the whole) to the consideration of 'New Man—New Values.' For those who have perceived the need of inward regeneration it is precisely such efforts as that of Florence Allshorn to create in individuals a new fundamental attitude to life that contain the seeds of fresh growth, and it is on these that any real hopes for the future must be based.

Behind all questions of human relations lies the ultimate question of man's existence, whether there is beyond all his strivings a Goodness and Perfection in the universe itself towards which he may climb and a Love in which he may trust, or whether he has nothing to rely on except his own strength and wisdom and can find no value in the world that is not of his own making. The purpose which dominates the life of society to-day is the ambition of man to transform the world, society and himself by means of his science and technics. In so far as this endeavour is the exercise of the freedom and responsibility with which man has been endowed by the Creator, there is no reason to quarrel with it. But it makes the whole difference whether he engages in the task in self-sufficiency and pride or in the knowledge that he is a partner with God in His work of creation. If man is in truth a created being, intended to live and work in partnership with God, he does violence to his essential nature when he forgets that fact, and his efforts are likely to meet with repeated and multiplying frustration unless they are redeemed and purified by the humility that is born of worship. It is in relation to this ultimate and supreme question that Florence Allshorn's life has its deepest significance. It was a life that in an outstanding degree makes it easier for other people to believe in God.

Florence once said in conversation that now and again an age throws up some person who is in a peculiar degree significant in relation to that period. She would have been the very last to imagine that she herself could conceivably be such a person. Yet who can freely open his mind to what she saw and was, and escape the feeling that the message of her life has just that peculiar relation to the needs and problems of our time? What she has left us is not an abstract doctrine or intellectual view, but a fresh vision of what it means to live.

The question is how far there are receptive minds able to absorb what she has to give. She once remarked that, while she believed that most of the students who passed through her hands during her twelve years of missionary training had received some help, she wondered whether as many as half-a-dozen had really *heard* her. To hear precisely what she had to say needs attentive listening. We mistake her meaning if we generalize about the practice and efficacy of love outside the direct relations of persons with persons. Florence with her stark realism never did this. She thought in terms of Christ's illustrations of leaven, of salt, of a light shining in the surrounding darkness. Her ceaseless concern was that the salt should not lose its saltness, that the light should not be dimmed. We have failed to hear her if we deceive ourselves with high-sounding phrases which have no relation to our actual attitudes and actions. We have not heard her if we shrink from the cost of being made real. We have truly heard her only if, having ceased to care about ourselves, we live single-mindedly 'for God and the other' and religion becomes for us 'really a song'.